GLOBALVIEWPOINTS

| Religion

Other Books of Related Interest:

Issues on Trial
Free Speech

Personal Liberty

Opposing Viewpoints Series
Atheism

Civil Liberties

Islam

Islamic Militancy

Tibet

GLOBALVIEWPOINTS

Religion

Diane Andrews Henningfeld, Book Editor

GREENHAVEN PRESS
A part of Gale, Cengage Learning

GALE
CENGAGE Learning™

Detroit • New York • San Francisco • New Haven, Conn • Waterville, Maine • London

Christine Nasso, *Publisher*
Elizabeth Des Chenes, *Managing Editor*

© 2010 Greenhaven Press, a part of Gale, Cengage Learning

Articles in Greenhaven Press anthologies are often edited for length to meet page requirements. In addition, original titles of these works are changed to clearly present the main thesis and to explicitly indicate the author's opinion. Every effort is made to ensure that Greenhaven Press accurately reflects the original intent of the authors. Every effort has been made to trace the owners of copyrighted material.

Cover image © Frederic Soltan/Sygma/Corbis.

LIBRARY OF CONGRESS CATALOGING-IN-PUBLICATION DATA

Religion / Diane Andrews Henningfeld, book editor.
p. cm. -- (Global viewpoints)
Includes bibliographical references and index.
ISBN 978-0-7377-4721-8 (hardcover) -- ISBN 978-0-7377-4722-5 (pbk.)
1. Religions. I. Henningfeld, Diane Andrews.
BL80.3.R425 2010
200.9--dc22
2009044184

Printed in the United States of America
1 2 3 4 5 6 7 14 13 12 11 10

Contents

Chapter 2: Religion, Science, and Education

Chapter 3: Religion and Politics

Chapter 4: Religion and Violence

Foreword

"The problems of all of humanity can only be solved by all of humanity."
—*Swiss author Friedrich Dürrenmatt*

Global interdependence has become an undeniable reality. Mass media and technology have increased worldwide access to information and created a society of global citizens. Understanding and navigating this global community is a challenge, requiring a high degree of information literacy and a new level of learning sophistication.

Building on the success of its flagship series, *Opposing Viewpoints*, Greenhaven Press has created the *Global Viewpoints* series to examine a broad range of current, often controversial topics of worldwide importance from a variety of international perspectives. Providing students and other readers with the information they need to explore global connections and think critically about worldwide implications, each *Global Viewpoints* volume offers a panoramic view of a topic of widespread significance.

Drugs, famine, immigration—a broad, international treatment is essential to do justice to social, environmental, health, and political issues such as these. Junior high, high school, and early college students, as well as general readers, can all use *Global Viewpoints* anthologies to discern the complexities relating to each issue. Readers will be able to examine unique national perspectives while, at the same time, appreciating the interconnectedness that global priorities bring to all nations and cultures.

Material in each volume is selected from a diverse range of sources, including journals, magazines, newspapers, nonfiction books, speeches, government documents, pamphlets, organization newsletters, and position papers. *Global Viewpoints* is truly global, with material drawn primarily from international sources available in English and secondarily from U.S. sources with extensive international coverage.

Features of each volume in the *Global Viewpoints* series include:

- An **annotated table of contents** that provides a brief summary of each essay in the volume, including the name of the country or area covered in the essay.

- An **introduction** specific to the volume topic.

- A **world map** to help readers locate the countries or areas covered in the essays.

- For each viewpoint, an **introduction** that contains notes about the author and source of the viewpoint explains why material from the specific country is being presented, summarizes the main points of the viewpoint, and offers three **guided reading questions** to aid in understanding and comprehension.

- **For further discussion** questions that promote critical thinking by asking the reader to compare and contrast aspects of the viewpoints or draw conclusions about perspectives and arguments.

- A worldwide list of **organizations to contact** for readers seeking additional information.

- A **periodical bibliography** for each chapter and a **bibliography of books** on the volume topic to aid in further research.

- A comprehensive **subject index** to offer access to people, places, events, and subjects cited in the text, with the countries covered in the viewpoints highlighted.

Global Viewpoints is designed for a broad spectrum of readers who want to learn more about current events, history, political science, government, international relations, economics, environmental science, world cultures, and sociology—students doing research for class assignments or debates, teachers and faculty seeking to supplement course materials, and others wanting to understand current issues better. By presenting how people in various countries perceive the root causes, current consequences, and proposed solutions to worldwide challenges, *Global Viewpoints* volumes offer readers opportunities to enhance their global awareness and their knowledge of cultures worldwide.

Introduction

"Religious freedom and the right to life are both protected by the fundamental law of most modern nations, including the United States. When one party asserts one right and the other party asserts the other, which should prevail?"

Connie Veneracion,
"Religion and Medicine,"
Manila Standard Today,
January 8, 2009.

During the first decade of the 21st century, an increasing number of cases illustrate the intersection of religious beliefs with the practice of medicine. In some cases, religious beliefs of a medical practitioner may prevent him or her from providing certain services to patients. In other cases, patients refuse services offered by medical care workers because the services violate their religious beliefs. Another issue, parents who refuse medical treatment for their children due to their beliefs, is particularly controversial. Finally, the religious beliefs of a community may be so strong that members of the community may commit violence against medical workers performing procedures or giving services prohibited by their religion.

For some doctors, nurses, and pharmacists, religious beliefs may stand in the way of providing services. For example, a doctor may refuse to perform an abortion on a woman even if the procedure is legal in the doctor's country. In another instance, a pharmacist may refuse to fill a prescription for birth control medication if his or her religion condemns premarital sex. As Iliya Englin writes in the September 2007 *Australian Doctor,* "The impact of religious beliefs on the delivery of care is more of an issue than it was a mere generation ago." Englin believes that doctors who refuse to perform certain services are still "valuable members of the community," but only if they are clear and honest with their patients from the beginning. The U.S. Department of Health and Human Services (HHS) issued a statement protecting the rights of health care workers who refuse to offer services based on religious conviction. In a news release from the HHS dated December 18, 2008, HHS secretary Mike Leavitt said, "Doctors and other health care providers should not be forced to choose between good professional standing and violating their conscience." On the other hand, while the beliefs of health care providers are respected in other countries, there are restrictions. For example, in the United Kingdom, where a doctor has the right to refuse to perform an abortion, instructions from the General Medical Council's *Personal Beliefs and Medical Practice* (March 2008) clearly state, "Where a patient who is awaiting or has undergone a termination of pregnancy needs medical care, you have no legal or ethical right to refuse to provide it on the grounds of a conscientious objection to the procedure."

The religious convictions of patients offer a second point of intersection and, at times, conflict within the medical community. Jehovah's Witnesses, for example, do not believe in blood transfusions. In many cases this can lead to the death of a patient. In England in 2003, Angela Shipperley died from complications of a cesarean delivery of her second child, largely because of her steadfast refusal to accept blood transfusions against the recommendations of her doctors. Catholics and evangelical Christians often do not believe that life support should be removed from patients, even if the patient has no hope for recovery. Emine Saner, in the March 2007 issue of the *Guardian* (a British newspaper), reports, "In 2003, the Association of Catholic Women started selling ID cards . . . that, in effect, ask doctors not to withdraw treatment if the patient is deemed to have a 'poor quality of life.'" The conflict between medical practice and religious beliefs, however, is no more contentious than in the cases of children who are seriously ill and whose parents do not want them to be treated because of religious beliefs. Daniel Hauser, for example, was a thirteen-year-old Minnesota boy who contracted Hodgkin's lymphoma in 2009. His family belonged to an American religious sect known as the Nemenhah Band and refused to allow him to receive chemotherapy as his doctors insisted. The case ultimately ended up in court, and a judge ruled that Hauser must receive the treatments. Wendy Cadge reports on a similar case in the June 16, 2009, issue of *Religion Dispatches*, in which a Wisconsin woman was found "guilty of second-degree reckless homicide for praying instead of seeking medical help while her eleven-year-old diabetic daughter Madeline died."

Medical treatment and religious beliefs also come into conflict when medical treatments confront the religious doctrine of organized religion or culturally held religious beliefs. In Brazil in 2009, a Catholic doctor was excommunicated for performing an abortion on a nine-year-old girl who had been raped by her stepfather and was pregnant with twins. The doctor believed that he was acting to save the child's life; Archbishop Don José Cardoso Sobrinho immediately excommunicated the doctor. The case caused significant controversy within the Catholic Church, with the top bioethics official from the Vatican publicly disagreeing with Sobrinho's decision.

In the most extreme cases, some religious people take the law into their own hands to prevent medical workers from performing certain procedures. In May 2009, Dr. George Tiller was shot to death at church by an antiabortion extremist. Tiller had been shot previously in 1993 by another antiabortion extremist, Rachelle Shannon. According to Frances Kissling in the May 31, 2009, issue of *Religion Dispatches*, "Shannon insisted at her trial that she had done no wrong, and since Dr. Tiller went back to work performing abortions the next day, she would have gone back to the clinic to do whatever she could to stop the murder of babies."

No clear-cut answers to any of these conflicts exist, and clashes between the medical community and religious groups will likely continue. The viewpoints in this volume trace a number of controversial issues important in the consideration of religion around the world, including the difficult intersection of religion, science, and education, the political consideration of religious beliefs, and the impact of religion on violence.

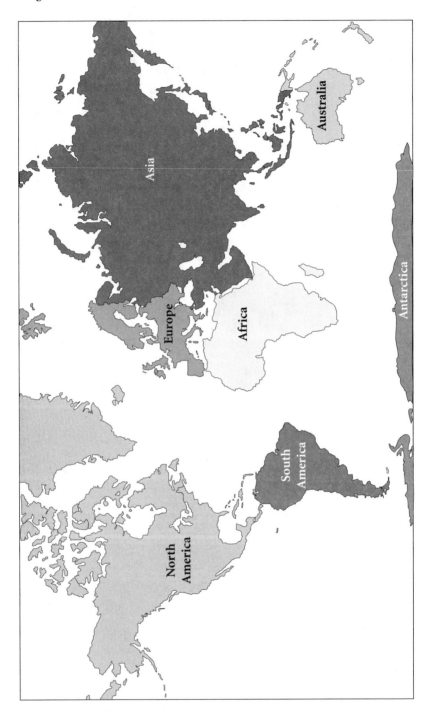

CHAPTER 1

Religious Developments Around the World

Pentecostal Christianity Is Growing Throughout the World

Pew Forum on Religion & Public Life

According to the Pew Forum on Religion & Public Life in the following viewpoint, the renewalist movement, composed of Pentecostal and other charismatic Christians, is growing rapidly throughout the world. A survey of Pentecostals and other charismatics in ten countries reveals the size of the movement. In addition, the survey describes the religious experience of renewalists, including divine healings, revelations, and exorcisms. Finally, the survey describes the influence the movement has on national politics, and touches on the moral codes to which Pentecostals and charismatics subscribe. The Pew Forum on Religion & Public Life is a nonpartisan, non-advocacy organization that provides information and analysis to public leaders.

A s you read, consider the following questions:

1. What are the three criteria used to categorize a respondent as "charismatic" on the Pew Forum on Religion & Public Life survey described in this viewpoint?

Pew Forum on Religion & Public Life, "Executive Summary," *Spirit and Power: A 10-Country Survey of Pentecostals*, October 5, 2006. Copyright © 2006 Pew Research Center. Reprinted with the permission of the Pew Research Center's Forum on Religion & Public Life, www.pewforum.org.

2. What percentage of Pentecostals in Kenya report that they have personally witnessed the divine healing of an injury or illness?

3. What percentage of Kenyan Pentecostals say that their government should make their country a Christian nation?

By all accounts, Pentecostalism and related charismatic movements represent one of the fastest-growing segments of global Christianity. According to the *World Christian Database*, at least a quarter of the world's 2 billion Christians are thought to be members of these lively, highly personal faiths, which emphasize such spiritually renewing "gifts of the Holy Spirit" as speaking in tongues, divine healing and prophesying.

Even more than other Christians, Pentecostals and other renewalists believe that God, acting through the Holy Spirit, continues to play a direct, active role in everyday life.

Despite the rapid growth of the renewalist movement in the last few decades, there are few quantitative studies on the religious, political and civic views of individuals involved in these groups.

"Even more than other Christians, Pentecostals and other renewalists believe that God, acting through the Holy Spirit, continues to play a direct, active role in everyday life."

To address this shortcoming, the Pew Forum on Religion & Public Life, with generous support from the Templeton Foundation, recently conducted surveys in 10 countries with sizeable renewalist populations: the United States; Brazil, Chile and Guatemala in Latin America; Kenya, Nigeria and South Africa in Africa; and India, the Philippines and South Korea in Asia. In each country, surveys were conducted among a random sample of the public at large, as well as among over-samples of Pentecostals and charismatics.

In this report, the term Pentecostal is used to describe individuals who belong to classical Pentecostal denominations, such as the Assemblies of God or the Church of God in Christ that were founded shortly after the famous Azusa Street Revival in the early 20th century, as well as those who belong to Pentecostal denominations or churches that have formed more recently, such as the Brazil-based Universal Church of the Kingdom of God.

Charismatics, by contrast, are a much more loosely defined group. The term generally refers to Christians who have experienced the "in-filling" of the Holy Spirit but who are not members of Pentecostal denominations. Indeed, most charismatics are members of mainstream Protestant, Catholic and Orthodox denominations. In the surveys, respondents were categorized as charismatic if they met one of three criteria: (1) they describe themselves as "charismatic Christians"; or (2) they describe themselves as "Pentecostal Christians" but do not belong to Pentecostal denominations; or (3) they say they speak in tongues at least several times a year but they do not belong to Pentecostal denominations.

"Renewalist" is used as an umbrella term throughout the report to refer to Pentecostals and charismatics as a group.

How Many Renewalists?

The surveys find that the size and composition of the renewalist population varies substantially from country to country, ranging from a low of 5% in the areas of India surveyed to a high of 60% in Guatemala. In every nation surveyed except India, at least 10% of the population can be described as renewalist; in three countries (Brazil, Guatemala and Kenya) membership in the renewalist movement approaches or exceeds 50%. In two countries (Kenya and Nigeria), Pentecostals outnumber charismatics. In every other country, by contrast, the renewalist movement is primarily charismatic in character, with charismatics outnumbering Pentecostals by a margin of at least two-to-one. Pentecostals are more concentrated in Latin America and Africa (where they range from 9% of the population in Chile to 33% in Kenya) than they are in the United States or Asia (where they range from 1% of the population in the areas of India surveyed to 5% in the U.S.).

The largest charismatic populations are in Brazil (34% of the population), Guatemala (40%) and the Philippines (40%). In several other countries, including the U.S., Chile, Kenya and South Africa, approximately one-in-five people are charismatic. Taken together, these findings confirm that members of renewalist movements can be found in sizeable numbers throughout the world.

In six of the 10 countries, the surveys find that renewalists account for a majority of the overall Protestant population. Indeed, in five nations (Brazil, Chile, Guatemala, Kenya and the Philippines) more than two-thirds of Protestants are either Pentecostal or charismatic. In Nigeria, renewalists account for six-in-ten Protestants.

Renewalist Distinctives

The surveys find that there are certain religious experiences and practices that differentiate Pentecostals, and, to a lesser degree, charismatics, from other Christians. In seven of the 10 countries surveyed, for instance, at least half of Pentecostals say that the church services they attend frequently include people practicing the gifts of the Holy Spirit, such as speaking in tongues, prophesying or praying for miraculous healing. These types of services are less common, but still relatively prevalent, among charismatics. By contrast, in most of the countries surveyed, only small numbers of nonrenewalist Christians report attending religious services where these sorts of religious experiences occur.

While many renewalists say they attend religious services where speaking in tongues is a common practice, fewer tend to say that they themselves regularly speak or pray in tongues. In fact, in six of the 10 countries surveyed, more than four-in-ten Pentecostals say they never speak or pray in tongues.

"In seven of the 10 countries surveyed ... at least half of Pentecostals say that the church services they attend frequently include people practicing the gifts of the Holy Spirit, such as speaking in tongues, prophesying or praying for miraculous healing."

In all 10 countries surveyed, large majorities of Pentecostals (ranging from 56% in South Korea to 87% in Kenya) say that they have personally experienced or witnessed the divine healing of an illness or injury. In eight of the countries (India and South Korea are the exceptions) majorities of Pentecostals say that they have received a direct revelation from God.

Pentecostals around the world also are quite familiar with exorcisms; majorities in seven of the 10 countries say that they personally have experienced or witnessed the devil or evil spirits being driven out of a person. Generally, fewer charismatics, and even fewer other Christians, report witnessing these types of experiences.

Intensity of Belief

In addition to their distinctive religious experiences, renewalists also stand out for the intensity of their belief in traditional Christian doctrines and practices. For instance, in eight of the 10 countries surveyed (all except the U.S. and Chile), majorities of nonrenewalist Christians believe that the Bible is the word of God and is to be taken literally, word for word; but this view is even more common among Pentecostals than among nonrenewalist Christians. Similarly, large majorities of all Christians, renewalists and nonrenewalists alike, believe that miracles still occur today as in ancient times. But this belief tends to be even more intense among Pentecostals and, to a lesser extent, charismatics than among nonrenewalist Christians.

Pentecostals also stand out, especially compared with nonrenewalist Christians, for their views on eschatology, or "the end times." In six countries, at least half of Pentecostals believe that Jesus will return to earth during their lifetime. And the vast majority of Pentecostals (more than 80% in each country) believe in "the rapture of the Church," the teaching that before the world comes to an end the faithful will be rescued and taken up to heaven. This belief is less common (though still widely shared) among charismatics, who in turn tend to express higher levels of belief in the rapture than do other Christians.

"Pentecostals' frequent attempts to spread the faith are consistent with their widespread belief that faith in Jesus Christ represents the exclusive path to eternal salvation."

Pentecostals also make a concerted effort to share their faith with non-believers. In eight of the 10 countries surveyed, majorities of Pentecostals say they share their faith with non-believers at least once a week. And relatively few Pentecostals say this is something they never do. Charismatics tend to be somewhat less likely than Pentecostals to share their faith on a weekly basis.

Pentecostals' frequent attempts to spread the faith are consistent with their widespread belief that faith in Jesus Christ represents the exclusive path to eternal salvation; in every country surveyed except South Korea, at least 70% of Pentecostals completely agree that belief in Jesus is the only way to be saved from eternal damnation.

Renewalists and Politics

Renewalist Christians' strong focus on the supernatural has led to the widespread perception that the movement is largely apolitical in outlook. Although renewalists are focused on spiritual matters, many also say there is a role for religion in politics and public life. In nine of the 10 countries surveyed, for instance, at least half of Pentecostals say that religious groups should express their views on day-to-day social and political questions; support for this position is equally wide-spread among charismatics. In every country surveyed, fur-thermore, renewalists are at least as likely as others to express this view.

Majorities of renewalists in every country surveyed say that it is important to them that their political leaders have strong Christian beliefs. In six of the 10 countries, at least three-quarters of Pentecostals share this view; in the other four countries, at least two-thirds of Pentecostals agree with this position. Charismatics, as well, share the conviction that political leaders should have strong Christian beliefs.

In seven of the 10 countries surveyed, majorities or plu-ralities of Pentecostals say there should be a separation be-tween church and state. But in each of these countries, size-able minorities of Pentecostals say that their government should take special steps to make their country a Christian country. And in three countries, including the U.S., Pentecos-tals who favor separation of church and state are at least slightly outnumbered by Pentecostals who say that the govern-ment should take special steps to make their nation a Chris-tian country.

Regionally, support for this position is particularly strong among Pentecostals in Africa, where 48% of Kenyan Pentecos-tals, 58% of Nigerian Pentecostals and 45% of South African Pentecostals say the government should take steps to make their nation a Christian nation. In every country, fewer than half of charismatics express support for the idea that their government should take steps to make their country a Christian nation.

"More than half (52%) of American Pentecostals say that the government should take special steps to make the U.S. a Christian country, compared with only 25% among Christians overall."

In many of the 10 countries surveyed, large majorities of the general population hold quite conservative positions on several social and moral issues. But even in these generally conservative countries, Pentecostals often stand out for their traditional views on a wide range of social and moral issues, from homosexuality to extramarital sex to alcohol consumption. Majorities of Pentecostals in nine countries (all except the U.S.), for example, say that drinking alcohol can never be justified. In six of the 10 countries, majorities of Pentecostals say the same thing about divorce.

In most of the countries surveyed (all except the U.S. and South Korea), large majorities of the general population say that abortion can never be justified, and renewalists tend to share this view. The percentage of Pentecostals who say that abortion can never be justified ranges from 64% in the U.S. to 97% in the Philippines. Similarly, the percentage of charismatics who say that abortion is never justified ranges from 57% in the U.S. to 96% in the Philippines.

Renewalists in the United States

The patterns of religious belief and practice that set renewalists apart from other Christians around the world also apply to Pentecostals and charismatics in the United States. In the U.S., for instance, roughly two-thirds of Pentecostals and charismatics report attending church at least weekly, compared with less than half for the population as a whole. And the religious services attended by U.S. renewalists tend to be quite different from the ones attended by others; more than half of U.S. Pentecostals who report attending church say that the services they attend frequently include people speaking in tongues and manifesting other signs of the Spirit; the same is true for roughly three-in-ten charismatic church attenders in the U.S. Other U.S. Christians are much less familiar with this type of church service.

U.S. renewalists, like renewalists around the world, also often stand out for their moral conservatism. Eight-in-ten U.S. Pentecostals say that homosexuality is never justified, for instance, and nearly six-in-ten charismatics share this view. Among the public as a whole, by contrast, roughly half say homosexuality can never be justified. Renewalists in the U.S. also are more likely than others to oppose drinking alcohol.

And just as renewalists around the world favor a role for religion in public life, the same holds true for renewalists in the U.S. For instance, nearly eight-in-ten American Pentecostals (79%) say that religious groups should express their views on day-to-day social and political questions, compared with 61% of the public as a whole. And more than half (52%) of American Pentecostals say that the government should take special steps to make the U.S. a Christian country, compared with only 25% among Christians overall.

Other Findings

In addition to these results, the 10-nation survey also finds:

- In most countries, Pentecostals tend to be somewhat more hopeful than nonrenewalist Christians about their future financial prospects.

- Pentecostals are divided on the question of whether or not AIDS is a punishment from God; majorities in three of the countries surveyed (Guatemala, Kenya and

South Korea) believe that AIDS is a punishment from God for immoral sexual behavior, but majorities of Pentecostals in five other countries explicitly reject this point of view.

- In most countries, Pentecostals are somewhat more likely than nonrenewalist Christians to sympathize more with Israel than with the Palestinians.

- Pentecostals in six of the countries surveyed are more willing than the public overall to allow women to serve as pastors or church leaders. This pattern, however, does not generally extend to other gender issues, where there is no consistent pattern differentiating Pentecostals from others.

- Majorities of Pentecostals in all 10 countries surveyed agree that God will grant good health and relief from sickness to believers who have enough faith, and in nine of the countries most Pentecostals say that God will grant material prosperity to all believers who have enough faith.

- Opinions about the U.S.-led war on terror vary substantially from country to country. In South Korea, for instance, only 16% of Pentecostals and 10% of charismatics say they favor U.S.-led efforts to fight terrorism. In the U.S. and the Philippines, by contrast, at least seven-in-ten Pentecostals (and nearly as many U.S. and Filipino charismatics) support U.S. efforts to fight terrorism.

Roadmap to the Report

These and many more findings are presented and discussed in more detail below. This report is divided into four main sections. Section I describes the religious experiences and beliefs of renewalists. The moral values and social attitudes of renewalists are presented and analyzed in Section II. Section III reports on their personal and social outlooks. Finally, Section IV describes the political views of renewalists, comparing them with the views held by other Christians in each of the 10 countries surveyed.

China Is Experiencing a Religious Revival

Paul Webster

In the following viewpoint, Paul Webster reports on the growth of religion in China, including Buddhism and Christianity. He notes that although the Chinese government officially is committed to atheism, it is nonetheless displaying tolerance for five state-recognized faiths: Buddhism, Taoism, Islam, Protestantism, and Catholicism. According to Webster, China's government intends to oversee the religious resurgence to promote national unity and manage the large flow of cash into religious temples. Webster is a reporter for the Canadian magazine Maclean's.

As you read, consider the following questions:

1. According to Master Jue Xing, quoted in this viewpoint, how were people educated about religion in the aftermath of the Cultural Revolution in China?

2. According to McGill University professor Kenneth Dean, what is the ratio of temples to villagers in operation in China?

3. According to Lin Guoping, quoted in this viewpoint, why should China have a flexible religion policy?

Paul Webster, "Go Forth and Pray, Comrade: History's Largest Religious Revival Is Unfolding in China and the Government Is Smiling on It," *Maclean's*, vol. 121, no. 32, August 18, 2008, pp. 38–39. Copyright © 2008 by Rogers Publishing Ltd. Reproduced by permission.

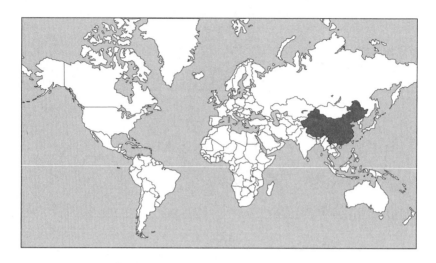

On almost any day, the scene outside Shanghai's Jade Buddha Temple could easily be confused with a major celebrity event. Limousines compete for curb space, and sophisticated urbanites line up with tourists as well as peasants and workers from every region of China to purchase tickets. Inside the temple's ochre yellow walls, its abbot, Master Jue Xing, revels as he glides through the throngs. Less than a decade ago, the 25-year-old temple he administers in Shanghai's booming core remained a ransacked relic of anti-religious purges. Today, thanks to donations from hundreds of newly wealthy devotees, it's thriving. As clouds of incense smoke rise from an enormous bronze brazier and saffron-robed monks softly chant traditional prayers, the richly lacquered altars glow in the late afternoon sun. Sweeping his hand across the panorama, Jue offers a thought that just a few years ago would have seemed ludicrous in a country governed by atheistic Communists with a long history of repression. "This is a golden time for religion in China," he pronounces.

A member of the Chinese Communist Party's central committee and one of the country's most powerful Buddhist leaders, Jue, at age 38, has already been a monk for 22 years. He recalls the aftermath of the decade-long Cultural Revolution era. "We were educated to see religion as opium, as superstition," recalls Jue, who entered a monastery as a child only a few years after the religious purges of the '70s ended. Through the '80s and '90s, China remained barren ground. Now the rebirth of Shanghai's preeminent Buddhist temple as a glittering showcase for a religion with an estimated 400 million followers and a billion sympathizers is evident in its bricks and mortar: "A few years ago the government moved a hospital to allow us to expand," Jue says. "If the government was afraid of us they would not let us expand. And we plan to keep expanding."

Buddhism, Taoism and Christianity Are Growing

The miracle at Shanghai's Jade Buddha Temple is far from an isolated affair. Across China, popular fervour for Buddhism is swelling. At the newly restored Fa Zang Jiang Temple in Shanghai's market quarter, where lives of monastic austerity are now leavened by comforts such as air conditioning in the eating hall, temple master Guan Hui says the situation is unlike anything he could have imagined 20 years ago. "In the 1970s we only had 30 or 40 temples here in Shanghai. In the 1990s, there were 70. After 2000 there were more than 80." Temple reconstruction is big business in other parts of the country as well. In the villages of central Fujian province, for instance, a recent survey by McGill University professor Kenneth Dean estimates that there is now one temple in operation for every 350 villagers; residents can attend 250 days of religious celebration a year. China's main Buddhist and Taoist sites and festivals are overrun with crowds of pilgrims.

Christianity, too, is booming, with an estimated one million new followers joining congregations annually. More Protestants attend church on Sundays in China than in western Europe, Protestantism's historic heartland, scholars say. Although the government severely restricts missionary activities, many American evangelical churches see China as a new frontier even more promising than Africa and the former Soviet Union.

Business Freedom Leads to Religious Freedom

Seen just by the numbers, China's religious reawakening can be called the largest religious resurgence in human history. It's "a social transformation completely unprecedented in the history of world," says James Miller, a professor of Chinese religions at Queen's University. Like many observers, he thinks China's economic liberalization is powering the resurgence. Freedom of belief partly flows from business freedom, Miller says. Growing numbers of China's hundreds of thousands of new millionaires seem anxious to credit the traditional gods for their good fortune—to thank them and, perhaps, to acquire further blessings. "An old Chinese adage says, 'Three feet above the head there are gods,'" explains Ye Xiaowen, a former scholar who now charts China's increasingly relaxed official policies as the country's minister of religion. "Even when Chinese people are not religious," he explains, "when they look up, three feet above there are gods."

Coming from the mouth of a minister, this is remarkable. Beijing maintains an ideological commitment to atheism as a central tenet of Marxism; the government is famous for acts of religious repression, most notably involving the Falun Gong, a movement fusing elements of Buddhism, Taoism and Confucianism. But Ye's new attitude reflects a broader shift. In November [2007], at a major meeting of top Communist officials from across the country before the run-up to the Olympics, President Hu Jintao listed the Chinese government's top strategic priorities. Among the top five: managing the religious resurgence. That decision delighted Ye, whose status within the government has rapidly escalated since he took over his then-obscure ministry 16 years ago. Sporting a tie promoting the Beijing Olympics, Ye drove home a tolerant message. "If a society is to be a healthy one," he said, "there must be different ideas within it, including religious and non-religious beliefs, including different religions, including Buddhists and Christians." Then, in slightly stilted English, Ye added a rather revisionist assertion. "Our respect for freedom of religion," he intoned, "is deeply rooted in our cultural history."

"Seen just by the numbers, China's religious reawakening can be called the largest religious resurgence in human history."

On the eve of the Beijing Olympics, Ye is not alone among Chinese officials genuflecting toward human rights concerns in the face of grave evidence to the contrary. As Ye himself notes, "There are some problems, but foreign friends shouldn't worry about it. Our country is building a harmonious society." Then, after describing unregistered Christian sects as "wolves in the herd," in time-honoured Chinese tradition, the minister blamed junior officials in the provinces, suggesting that problems with religious freedom can mostly be traced to the failure of local officials to respect national laws.

Religious Tolerance Is a Strategic Move

No surprise, China's newfound tolerance is a strategic move. With floods of Chinese seeking spiritual solace, new government policies aim to use religion to promote national unity. "Religions should propel development and service social equality as much as possible, instead of causing problems," Ye said. "As the economy prospers, people become agitated. The people need religious beliefs to support themselves." According to analysts such as Miller, Beijing hopes China's rising religious fervour will help cement national harmony at a time of growing unrest and division between urban and rural

Many Chinese Are Religious

Religious observance in China is on the rise. According to a survey published in a state-run newspaper, 31.4 percent of Chinese adults are religious, a figure that is three times the initial government estimate. The Chinese Communist Party (CCP) is officially atheist, but it has been growing more tolerant of religious activity for the past twenty years. China's constitution explicitly allows "freedom of religious belief," and in 2005, the State Council passed new guidelines broadening legal rights for state-sanctioned groups. . . .

But religious freedom is still not universal in China. The state only recognizes five official religions—Buddhism, Taoism, Islam, Catholicism, and Protestantism—and considers the practice of any other faith illegal. Religious organizations are required to register with one of five state-sanctioned patriotic religious associations, each of which is supervised by the State Administration for Religious Affairs (SARA). Religious groups that fail to affiliate with one of the five official religions are denied legal protection under Chinese law.

Preeti Bhattacharji,
"Backgrounder: Religion in China, Council on Foreign Relations,"
May 16, 2008. www.cfr.org.

people, and rich and poor. "There is a crisis of belief in China. People used to believe in communism. But that isn't the case anymore," Miller argues. "People are looking for alternatives. Religion is one of these. The government is using religion as a kind of lever to promote nationalism, to promote Chinese culture, and to prop up its own support."

Religion can serve other needs. In Fujian province, on China's south coast, for instance, folk faiths that are thousands of years old are flourishing amid a spree of temple restoration. The Chinese government is supportive partly because Fujian folk faiths spread long ago to Taiwan and elsewhere in Asia, explains Lin Guoping, a professor of religion at Fuzhou University. "We need Taiwanese investment and overseas Chinese investment. That's why we have a flexible religion policy. Religion builds bridges." That analysis draws an echo from Jing Yin, a Buddhist monk who directs the University of Hong Kong Centre of Buddhist Studies. "The government gradually understands that diversity of faiths is very important," says Jing, "and also that it is useful for economic development."

"With floods of Chinese seeking spiritual solace, new government policies aim to use religion to promote national unity."

The Chinese Government Controls the Religious Resurgence

It's worth noting that China has a political history in which religious revolts—led by Buddhist, Taoist and other sects—have often helped to trigger dramatic regime change, including the late-19th-century unravelling of China's last dynastic regime. And so lawmakers have expertly circumscribed religious freedom. Only five faiths—Buddhism, Taoism, Islam, Protestantism and Catholicism—are legal. All forms of religious observance and debate are limited by lengthy lists of forbidden activities. Religious festivals are closely monitored by overwhelming numbers of police. The masters of the temples may be monks, but they answer to masters of a wholly different type in Beijing.

In fact, Ye says, the sudden surge in religious fervour, and the flood of cash into the temples, justifies government intervention in every aspect of Chinese religious life. "Money flows ceaselessly into the temples," Ye notes. "In the past, people went to the temple to burn incense sticks, and the temples could not earn money." Now, because of the problem of "overflowing money," the minister says, "monks have to accept supervision after getting rich. They cannot become corrupt." Under this regime, the day still seems far off when the masters of the temples would dare raise political questions.

But Jing warns that government management of the religious resurgence may undermine the spiritual integrity of the temples and monasteries. He worries especially about the growing commercialism within many temples and of extensive business operations like those at Shanghai's Jade Buddha, which has a busy Web site and popular outreach programs. Under government stewardship, other famous Buddhist sites like those on [Mount] Putuo Island, home to many ancient monasteries, are being redeveloped around massive new hotel and temple complexes. "The market economy is seriously hurting the religious nature of the monasteries," says Jing. "Little time has been spent on teaching and meditation, to the extent that the core religious functions of monasteries are in danger of becoming merely decorative."

"Under government stewardship . . . famous Buddhist sites . . . are being redeveloped around massive new hotel and temple complexes."

For Chinese Buddhists with roots in the faith going back through the centuries, the changes are astonishing. Zhang Jin Guo, a 58-year-old Buddhist who lives in a two-room house and works in a temple park on [Mount] Putuo Island as a gatekeeper, says although the changes are ruining some of the island's charm, he welcomes Buddhism's change of fortune. "I'm happy that more and more people now believe in Buddha," he explained on a stroll along the beach with his six-year-old granddaughter and her friends. And government policy, he suggests, can't entirely control religion. "During the

Cultural Revolution, all the temples here were destroyed. They destroyed the Buddhas. But we still prayed."

In New Zealand, Buddhism Is Experiencing Rapid Growth

Vanessa Walker

In the following viewpoint, Vanessa Walker reports that a wide variety of people in New Zealand have chosen to follow the Buddhist faith in increasing numbers. Walker suggests that the ethical message of Buddhism is what has attracted so many people from so many different backgrounds. The viewpoint also points out that while some Buddhist converts accept all Buddhist teachings, others pick and choose among the Buddhist beliefs that seem most reasonable to them. Walker is the author of Mantras & Misdemeanours: An Accidental Love Story *and the former religious affairs writer for the* Australian.

As you read, consider the following questions:

1. How have the Friends of the Western Buddhist Order attempted to indigenize their centers?
2. What is the dharma, according to this viewpoint?
3. How many books on Buddhism has Scott Wong accumulated in decades of study, according to the viewpoint?

Thousands of New Zealanders from all walks of life have one thing in common: They are followers of Buddhism.

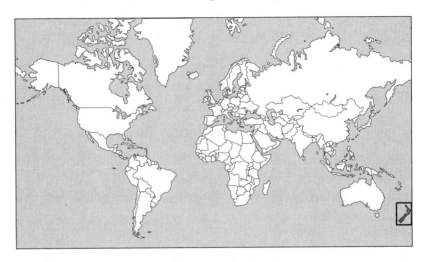

Twenty-four years ago, Charlotte Wrightson used to thrash around angrily in an Auckland punk band called The Plague, making a commotion about the evils of private property, capitalism and conformity.

Around the same time, in Hong Kong, businessman Scott Wong had a recurring dream that led him to question the monks at a monastery he would visit during business trips on the mainland.

Going back further, to the mid-1970s, Simon Harrison was studying pure mathematics at Oxford University and living in a "free-thinking" house in Britain when he met someone who changed the course of his life.

Disparate People, Connected by Faith

Today [2007] these seemingly disparate people are connected by a faith that is growing quietly in New Zealand. According to the latest census 52,394 people identified themselves as Buddhist—an increase of nearly 11,000 since 2001. That's small compared with the 2 million-strong Christian population, but deduct the 37,590 Buddhists who brought their beliefs with them when they migrated here, mainly from Asia, and it emerges nearly 15,000 New Zealanders have converted to Buddhism, a faith with which they have little evident connection. Buddhism is the largest religion apart from Christianity and Hinduism (nearly 64,000), and outsizes all the religions that attract more attention, such as Islam (approximately 36,000), Brethren (18,000) and Scientology (357).

And many more are curious about its fundamental message. When one of Buddhism's most visible adherents, the Nobel Prize-winning Dalai Lama, last month [June 2007] made his fourth visit to New Zealand, 10,400 people who filled Auckland's Vector Arena and 4300 in Wellington's TSB Arena paid to hear him talk. Peel back the numbers and it transpires New Zealand hosts the gamut of Buddhist traditions from monks living in semi-silent solitude in a forest valley in Wellington, to Zen adherents trying to penetrate their innermost consciousness using koan (paradoxical questions that cannot be answered by the discursive intellect), to outwardly ordinary people taking up meditating and seeking instruction from Tibetan lamas on how to liberate oneself from the cycle of birth and death.

"According to the latest census 52,394 people identified themselves as Buddhist—an increase of nearly 11,000 since 2001."

There are small thriving nunneries that, in style and substance, are indistinguishable from their counterparts in Asia, but there are also Buddhist groups such as Friends of the Western Buddhist Order who have attempted to modernise Buddhism and indigenise their centres with kauri and puriri trees. Auckland has the country's largest Buddhist temple, an ornate 3.6ha complex that resembles a small town and provides almost as many services as such to its thousands of attendees.

The Five Ethical Tenets

What unites these groups are the five ethical tenets: not killing, not stealing, refraining from sexual misconduct, not using harmful speech and not taking intoxicants that cloud the mind. Further pledges include not gossiping about the faults of others; not praising oneself and disparaging others; not to withhold spiritual or material aid but to practise generosity: not to become angry but to practise forbearance and to uphold the Buddhist way.

Buddhists believe not in divine intervention but in the law of cause and effect (karma), in reincarnation, and that the path to enlightenment is achieved through an individual's thought transformation. For the New Zealanders who have converted to Buddhism, it is less a religious label than a cohesive set of principles to help them navigate life.

Former punk Charlotte Wrightson—who once played naked except for a coating of yellow paint at the Nambassa rock festival—is now 47-year-old Zen priest Amala Wrightson. She established the Auckland Zen Centre, a collection of three draughty rooms at the former Sanitarium Factory in Royal Oak. Here some 40 practitioners—ranging from Westerners, Asians, Eastern Europeans and Americans—take instruction from her. A further 300 subscribe to the group's mailing list.

"Buddhists believe not in divine intervention but in the law of cause and effect (karma), in reincarnation, and that the path to enlightenment is achieved through an individual's thought transformation."

As is the case with many people who have adopted Buddhism, Wrightson's transformation began when she was in her 20s and faced her first big life challenge. She was raised an Anglican, and her then boyfriend, now husband, poet Richard von Sturmer, had gone on what was supposed to be an exciting trip to Italy to study at a reputable theatre school. "But it sort of ended up being a crisis year. We had trouble finding a place to live and we ended up in a cold room looking after the son of the theatre director. Richard got writer's block and suffered from insomnia," she says. "That made us realise we needed to get a bit more sorted out in terms of our ability to cope with things."

Beginning a New Life

By chance one of the books they took with them was *The Three Pillars of Zen*. It precipitated a trip to Stockholm to hear author Roshi Philip Kapleau speak and that led Wrightson to her first three-week retreat in 1988. For the former punk the routine was strenuous; participants rose at 4:30 A.M.: Their meditation and work was conducted in silence, interrupted only by simple meals until they fell into bed at 9:30 P.M..

But the intense singularity of the experience opened up her mind. "I remember going into the dormitory bathroom to brush my teeth and turning on the tap and hearing the water as if for the first time. I realized how much noise there usually was in my mind, that normally I don't live or experience my life.

"Just a little thing like that gave me faith to keep going. It's not always like that—often it's just a struggle—but I got a sense of how effective the practice was."

For the next 15 years, Wrightson and her husband lived between New Zealand and Roshi Kapleau's centre in upstate New York. In 1999 Wrightson became a Zen priest, making the study and teaching of Buddhism her life's vocation. Being a priest means she can remain married because unlike nuns she has not taken a vow of celibacy. She returned to New Zealand in 2003 to establish the centre.

Wrightson acknowledges there are varying levels of dedication from those who say they are Buddhist, but says most of her students are seriously studying the dharma (Buddha's teachings). "Zen is not as exotic as other traditions because

Changes in New Zealand's Five Largest Religions

Religious Affiliation	Number of Adherents: 1991 Census	Number of Adherents: 2006 Census	Population Change: Percentage
Christian	2,272,707	2,027,418	−11%
Maori Christian	56,055	65,550	+17%
Hindu	18,036	64,392	+257%
Buddhist	12,762	52,362	+311%
Islam	6,096	36,072	+490%

TAKEN FROM: *Statistics New Zealand*, 1991 and 2006 Censuses. www.stats.govt.nz.

you basically get told to go and sit and face a wall," she says. "The emphasis in Zen is on direct experience not the theory."

Buddhism, she says, has benefited her enormously. "I'm able to stay on an even keel through life's ups and downs. More able to really be with other people and help other people, I hope. I have a little bit more clarity and direction." Yet her decision to dedicate her life to the Zen path hasn't come without sacrifices—the hardest, she says, was the decision not to have children. "I couldn't have done what I've done if I had them. You can't do everything. There are points where you have to leave something behind."

Buddhism Appeals to a Diverse Group

Hugh Kemp is a Victoria University student who is writing his PhD thesis on Buddhism in New Zealand. A Christian who was raised in India, he recently traversed the country interviewing Buddhists from all walks of life to find why it appeals to such a diverse range of people.

He says immigrants find some degree of cultural solace in the traditional Buddhist rituals, as well as an identity which connects them to their country of origin. Those who have converted to Buddhism are largely Pakeha [New Zealanders of

European ancestry] (although he notes there are 1836 Maori [indigenous New Zealanders] Buddhists), baby-boomers in their 40s and 50s, many of whom have a "cut and paste" approach to the beliefs rather than wholesale adoption of its teachings. It is possible to blend Buddhism with secular life and other religions; there are, for example, Jewish and Catholic Buddhists who see the dharma as an additional facet to their lives, not a contradiction.

"[Converts] especially use meditation as a tool to cope with the crazy mixed-up world we live in," Kemp says. "A lot of people also told me that they find that it gives them an opportunity to take responsibility for their own spiritual development, unlike some other religions—and they also like the fact there is no overarching hierarchy."

"It is possible to blend Buddhism with secular life and other religions; there are, for example, Jewish and Catholic Buddhists who see the dharma [Buddha's teachings] as an additional facet to their lives, not a contradiction."

He believes the seeds of Buddhism's growth began with travelers to Asia during the 1960s and '70s. "My hunch is that Kiwis [New Zealanders] travelling through Asia had an exotic attraction to Buddhism. As a mindset, New Zealanders are curious and like differentness. Also we tend to support the underdog, hence the anti-nuclear thing with the US and we also think Tibet should not be bullied by China." He believes that among the attractions of New Zealanders to the Dalai Lama's Tibetan tradition, there is a strong political nuance. Many also talk about the charisma of the lamas.

One Man's Story

Simon Harrison is a case in point. He was instrumental in bringing the Dalai Lama to New Zealand this time, the culmination of a dramatic meeting as a 22-year-old with a Tibetan lama.

It was 1976 and Harrison was studying pure mathematics at Oxford University. As a mathematician he always had a question about how love, compassion and altruism fit into logic so a friend took him to a Buddhist centre. There he learned its logical basis but "on the last day [a Tibetan teacher called] Lama Yeshe came up the path. I was on the lawn and he simply said 'good morning' and that was love and compassion without needing any explanation," he says. "Meeting Lama Yeshe was the point at which I could never let go and it has sustained me since."

This is the essence of the lamas' significance in Buddhist practice—the simplest of exchanges can have a resonance beyond the ordinary. For Harrison, the seemingly mundane conversation became something much more significant; Lama Yeshe seemed the embodiment of goodness.

"Like many others, [businessman Simon Harrison] was attracted to Buddhism because of its promise of overall happiness."

For 25 years Harrison has worked as secretary and treasurer of Auckland's Dorje Chang Institute, a Tibetan Buddhist centre, while building up a successful business. He meditates for 40 minutes each morning, has an altar in his study and is a vegetarian who tries not to kill insects, spiders and other sentient beings. As a supply chain consultant for companies such as Fonterra [an exporter of dairy products], he says he hasn't had to struggle with being a Buddhist in corporate life. "There are parts of corporate life I don't get into, such as drinking parties, but I feel that as much as possible I maintain my ethics given my work. In sales situations, sometimes people have wanted me to say things that I didn't want to but I've found it more effective to be honest. The aspect of karma that I live my life by is personal responsibility and that means I cannot get away from the consequences of my actions."

He has turned down projects such as working for Tegel Chicken as well as excusing himself from working on a meat industry project. "But at the same time I have worked on projects for New Zealand breweries."

Like many others he was attracted to Buddhism because of its promise of overall happiness, a state he has achieved. But despite its benefits he says there are aspects that remain a struggle.

Scepticism and Belief

"Scepticism will always be a hallmark of western philosophical thought and wherever it came from I'll always have it with me," Harrison says. He cites the Tibetan Buddhist practice of guru devotion, whereby after having accepted someone as . . . [his or her] primary teacher a student must view him or her as an enlightened Buddha, doing whatever is asked of . . . [him or her] because the guru can comprehend its eventual spiritual benefit.

"With guru devotion you have to put scepticism aside. I understand why that's necessary, I just can't do it. So what I end up doing is offering service through administration, such as organising the Dalai Lama's visit."

During that trip Harrison arranged for Amala Wrightson to meet the Buddhist leader and ask for his blessing to set up New Zealand's first Buddhist Council. She has approached various Buddhist groups in the hope that for the first time Buddhists can contribute to issues such as the government's current review of immigration policy and the move to introduce education about all religions into schools.

In contrast, 55-year-old Scott Wong professes to 100 percent faith in the teachings. A teacher at the Tsi Ming temple in Greenlane, he decided to investigate Buddhism after a recurring dream featuring various Buddhist symbols. Then living in Hong Kong, he approached the monks at a temple on the Chinese mainland to decipher its meaning and began to inquire about Buddhist beliefs.

His path was slow and laborious, thoroughly investigating Buddha's teachings every step of the way. A retired business-man, he had started studying the basic tenets, taking three years to finish reading and understanding the seminal Mahayana text Path to Enlightenment. It took him one-and-a-half years to study the five precepts, making sure he understood exactly what they required of him. In decades of study he has accumulated 4000 books on Buddhism. He spends around six hours on study and four hours reciting mantras, meditating and studying the sutras (Buddhist scripture) every day. Through an interpreter he says the main benefits are simply in his thoughts and clarity of mind. "My mind has broadened so I have a wider perspective and a clearer picture. My heart and body are relaxed. I feel light, not burdened."

Filipinos Seek Greater Understanding of Muslims

Bernardo M. Villegas

In the following viewpoint, Bernardo M. Villegas argues that the image of Muslims as terrorists is an unfair one and that the majority of Muslims are peace-loving people. He draws on his own experience as a university teacher in the Philippines and states that his Christian and Muslim students practice similar virtues. He urges his fellow citizens to increase their understanding of Islam and to admire the way Muslims practice their faith. Villegas is the dean of the School of Economics at the University of Asia and the Pacific in Manila, Philippines.

As you read, consider the following questions:

1. What Islamic leader condemned Muslim protests against a conference planned by the Carmelite Center?
2. What document reflects the fact that Islam is compatible with human justice, according to Bernard M. Villegas?
3. Who should fast during Ramadan, according to Villegas?

It is unfortunate that the Taliban executed one of the 23 South Korean missionaries in Afghanistan. Such violent acts tend to support the unfair image that Muslims have gotten in many parts of the world, especially since the September 11, 2001 World Trade Center carnage. The truth of the matter is

Bernardo M. Villegas, "Greater Understanding of Muslims," *Manila Bulletin*, August 10, 2007. Copyright © 2007 *Manila Bulletin*. All rights reserved. Reproduced by permission.

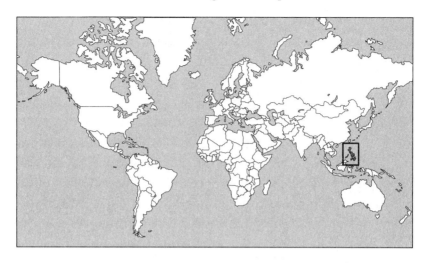

that the vast majority of Muslims all over the world are peace-loving and decent human beings. A recent survey [2007] conducted by the Pew Research Center of the United States clearly showed that the popular support given to Osama bin Laden and his strategies of violence have fallen precipitously in the Muslim world. The findings show that the percentage of Muslims who consider the suicide attacks as justified in defense of Islam has declined by as much as fifty percent the last two years in Lebanon, Bangladesh, Pakistan and Indonesia. The research, which was carried out through a survey in 47 countries, shows a clear decline in the acceptance of extremism among the Muslims, six years after the September 11 [2001] attacks, although the image of the United States continues to be negative, considered as a military threat.

Fundamentalists Do Not Speak for All Muslims

Closer to home, a recent [2007] event showing that Islamic fundamentalists do not speak for the whole Muslim world was that of an Islamic leader in Indonesia who condemned recent Muslim protests against a conference planned by the Carmelite center [a Catholic center] in West Java. Syafi'i Ma'arif, head of the Muhammadiyah, Indonesia's second largest Islamic organization, said that police must protect everyone's right to express his religious faith.

As reported by the ZENIT International News Agency last July 26 [2006], the Carmelite center, named Lembah Karmel Cikanyere, in Cianjur Regency, West Java, was forced to postpone an international conference as a result of pressure from demonstrators. Sister Lisa Martosudjito PKarm, the center's spokeswoman, said the conference's plan "essentially involved prayers and family meetings among lay Catholics" from Indonesia and abroad. After news of the postponement spread, Ma'arif responded that the police "should have moved against the radical Muslims, and stop their hostile actions against the Lembah Karmel Cikanyere."

"The rally has tarnished the good image of Islam. As Muslims, we know that Islam is a good, peaceful and loving religion," Ma'arif added. There is no good reason "to use and abuse (Islam) in an effort to legitimize harmful actions against other religious beliefs, to express dislike about them or conduct any unfriendly gestures" to scare Catholics, the Muslim scholar said. Sister PKarm expressed the Carmelite center's gratitude to the police, the military and moderate Muslims "who showed us friendship and protected our home from the demonstrators' threatening violence."

The Virtues and Values of Islam

For over forty years now, Muslim scholars and educators have been taking masteral courses in economics and education at the University of Asia and the Pacific in Manila. I have personally taught many of these Muslims and can attest to the fact that they practice in their daily lives the same virtues and values that Christians believe in. I still remember a Muslim female teacher who proclaimed to a large audience of educators attending a summer course at the Teachers Camp in Baguio that she became even a better Muslim after taking a course on values education at UA&P. She said that the values and virtues that we taught are exactly the same ones that Muslims are supposed to live: integrity, industry, sincerity, generosity and love for the poor, fidelity in marriage, loyalty in friendship, etc. In another instance, a Muslim male corrected the impression of his classmates that Muslim husbands ordinarily have four wives. He insisted that most Muslims believe in monogamy and that the only reason why some Muslim males have had more than one wife in the past was that in an extreme case, the prophet Muhammad permitted the marrying of several wives because the majority of the male population were decimated in a war. To repopulate the tribe, the prophet made this exception. But, according to this educator, the rule in Muslim societies is still monogamy.

"The values and virtues that we [Christians] taught are exactly the same ones that Muslims are supposed to live: integrity, industry, sincerity, generosity and love for the poor, fidelity in marriage, loyalty in friendship, etc."

In my experience dealing with Muslims, I have observed that they have the ten commandments clearly inscribed in their consciences and can distinguish between good and evil. The vast majority of them adhere to the precepts in which we believe, using passages from the Koran and their "hadiths" (tradition attributed to Muhammad) to justify the good things that they are obliged to perform. Unfortunately, a small minority of Muslims also use the Koran and Muslim tradition to justify their evil deeds. The few who want to kill innocent victims can also find phrases from the Koran that seem to justify their violent acts. This is the root of the confusion that the non-Muslim world can have of Islam. Since the Koran is not to be interpreted by any Supreme Authority whose word is infallible, every one ends up giving his own interpretation. Luckily, the vast majority of Muslims interpret the Koran in a way

---

Religious Affiliation in the Philippines

Christian:	92.6% (total of all Christians)
Roman Catholic	81.0%
Protestant	7.3%
Iglesia ni Kristo	2.3%
Aglipayan	2.0%
Muslim	5.1%
Buddhist	.1%
Others (includes tribal religions)	1.7%
None/Do not know	.5%

TAKEN FROM: 2000 Philippine Census. www.census.gov.ph/data/
pressrelease/cent-qs.html.

---

that is compatible with human justice and universal charity. The most outstanding document reflecting this fact was the Declaration on Human Rights in Islam signed in Cairo by 45 Ministers of Foreign Affairs of the Organisation of the Islamic Conference in 1990.

Five Fundamental Precepts

One cannot but admire the manner in which the good Muslims faithfully practise their religion. They adhere to five fundamental precepts:

1. The profession of Faith: There is no God other than Allah and Muhammad is His prophet.

2. Prayer: Five times a day in the direction of Mecca.

3. Almsgiving: Collected as a tax imposed by the Government so that the fund can be used for the benefit of Islam.

4. Fasting: Those who have reached majority age and are not aging or pregnant women. During the month of the Ramadan, nothing should be eaten or drunk during the day. There should be a total abstinence from food and drink, as well as matrimonial relations. The fasting starts

with the rising of the sun. For each day that the fasting is broken intentionally, a slave must be freed, or there must be two succeeding months of fasting or 60 indigent persons must be fed.

Dr. José Morales, an expert on Islam from the University of Navarra in Spain, wrote the following lines in one of [his] books: "One cannot forget that Islam is also the spiritual home of millions of men and women who practise a simple religiosity. They are in general multitudes who live with meekness a humble earthly existence. They are poor with a great zeal for justice, and for this reason are loved by God. Islam is a civilization peopled by good people." I am sure that all of us who have dealt with our Muslim brothers and sisters in the Philippines can fully support the words of Dr. Morales.

In the United States, Efforts at Jewish-Muslim Understanding Increase

Allan C. Brownfeld

In the following viewpoint, Allan C. Brownfeld writes about the growing dialogue between Jewish and Muslim congregations through organizations such as the Foundation for Ethnic Understanding. In addition, Brownfeld points out that the ambassador to the United States from Bahrain, an Arab country, is Jewish, an indication that dialogue between the two groups is possible. Finally, he asserts that Muslims and Jewish people have a long history of cooperation and helping each other, most notably during the Second World War. He urges readers to view the Palestinian-Israeli conflict as political rather than religious. Brownfeld is an author and a newspaper columnist.

As you read, consider the following questions:

1. What classes did the Congregation Beth El and the Islamic Center of Maryland hold jointly?
2. What term would Daniel Spiro like to see replace the phrase "Judeo-Christian"?
3. What 1991 film told the story of Muslim aid to Jews during the Nazi occupation of Paris?

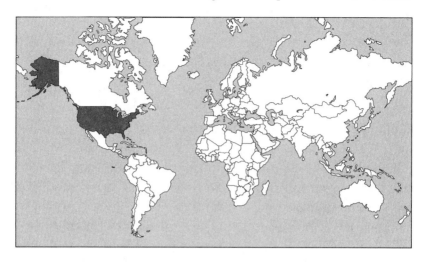

Despite the efforts of some Israelis and some in the American Jewish community to demonize the religion of Islam rather than focusing their attention on the minority of extremists within the Islamic community, efforts toward Muslim-Jewish understanding are growing.

Recalls Rabbi Bruce M. Lustig, senior rabbi at the Washington Hebrew Congregation, one of the largest Jewish congregations in North America with more than 3,000 families served: "Shortly after 9/11, I invited Bishop John Chane (Episcopal bishop of Greater Washington and the National Cathedral) and professor Akbar Ahmed (Ibn Khaldun scholar of Islamic studies at American University) to share with them the idea of starting an Abrahamic faith dialogue. My simple premise was based on what my mother told me as a child: Stay away from strangers. If these two men and their faiths were to remain strangers to me, I would only grow to fear them, not know them. Soon after, we held one of the first Abrahamic faith forums in America. We also forged a friendship that has been transformative. These men are my friends, my mentors, my sounding boards."

Teaching by Example

Although "we do not agree on every social or political question," Rabbi Lustig notes, "we have deep respect for, and a deep honesty with, each other. Having others challenge my ideas and demand clarity of creed is a powerful and uplifting experience. They have helped me to become a stronger Jew and a better rabbi. To my children, the answer to what it means to be Christian or Muslim is not abstract; it is the love they know from John and Akbar, who join us at our table and who teach us by example."

This past November [2008] more than 50 mosques and synagogues across the country participated in the Foundation for Ethnic Understanding's Weekend of Twinning.

With a stated premise that "we are all children of Abraham," the weekend brought together synagogues and mosques to combat Islamophobia and anti-Semitism in their communities.

"What we realized is that we don't know enough about each other," said Rabbi Gregory Harris of Congregation Beth El in Bethesda, Maryland. "We're relatives in the Abrahamic sense, but we're total strangers in every other sense of it."

Beth El paired with the Islamic Center of Maryland in Gaithersburg to hold "Judaism 101 and Islam 101" classes on the fundamentals of each religion.

"If we embrace what is beautiful in Islam and Muslims begin to embrace what is beautiful in Judaism, we can begin to produce a situation that might lead to peace."

According to Rabbi Marc Schneier, founder and president of the Foundation for Ethnic Understanding, who helped establish the weekend, the goal is to "create a paradigm of Jewish-Muslim support that we can export to other parts of the world . . . We must take advantage of these opportunities, especially within the Muslim world, where we are now beginning to see the emergence of a more moderate centrist voice that has a particular interest in reaching out to the Jewish religion."

Rabbi Schneier met in New York in November with King Abdullah of Saudi Arabia, a core supporter of the initiative.

The weekend fulfilled a pledge faith leaders took in 2007 at the World Conference on Dialogue in Madrid. Co-sponsors are the World Jewish Congress, the Muslim Public Affairs Council and the Islamic Society of North America.

Daniel Spiro, author of the novel *Moses the Heretic*, argues that the phrase Judeo-Christian should be replaced with "Abrahamic." He notes that although the world faces a real problem of Islamic terrorism, the religion also contains elements that are "uniquely beautiful," and that "We Jews need to seek them out. Most of us viscerally appreciate Christian ethics as a useful add-on to the foundation of Jewish ethics. But when we think about Islam, most of us don't appreciate what is profoundly beautiful. We basically see Islam as a violent outgrowth of monotheism. I want that changed."

In Spiro's view, "To borrow from another religion, if we want peace in Israel we need to generate good karma. If we embrace what is beautiful in Islam and Muslims begin to embrace what is beautiful in Judaism, we can begin to produce a situation that might lead to peace."

A Jewish Ambassador Represents an Arab Country

Consider the case of Houda Ezra Nonoo, who in July [2008] presented her credentials to President George W. Bush as Bahrain's ambassador to the U.S., making her the first Jew to represent an Arab country in Washington, DC.

In her first interview, with the Dec. 4, 2008 issue of *Washington Jewish Week*, Ambassador Nonoo explained: "Bahrain is an open and tolerant society and it doesn't matter what religion you are. I'm Jewish, but I'm also Bahraini. My grandfa-

A Rabbi Speaks About Jewish-Muslim Dialogue

In some ways, the challenge of interfaith dialogue is always the same—to reach beyond one's own comfort, one's own concerns, and one's own preconceptions, to listen deeply and generously to the experiences of others, to learn with and from them about ourselves and about each other.

But there are particular challenges—and opportunities—for those involved in Jewish-Muslim dialogue. Clearly, for Jews and Muslims, there is much mutual fear and mistrust to be overcome in our generation. The Israeli-Palestinian conflict looms large for both of our communities. . . . We have to have the courage to speak with each other honestly about Israel and Palestine, to challenge each other even as we challenge ourselves, to listen carefully without relinquishing our own dignity or the dignity of the other.

Sharon Cohen Anisfeld,
"The Efficacy of Jewish-Muslim Dialogue,"
The Center for Jewish-Muslim Relations, April 20, 2008.

ther served on the Municipality Council as early as 1934, so we've always been integrated into society."

In the late 1930s and early 1940s, as many as 1,500 Jews lived and prospered in Bahrain. "Things changed in 1948," according to *Washington Jewish Week*, "with the establishment of the state of Israel. Riots erupted, the sole synagogue was closed and most of Bahrain's Jews emigrated, leaving for Great Britain ... Currently, about 35 Jews live among Bahrain's 700,000 inhabitants. This is a constant source of pride for Bahraini officials ... In November, King Hamad bin Isa Al-Khalifa, during a meeting in New York, beseeched about 50 Bahraini Jewish expatriates to consider returning home—a move relatively unheard of in the rest of the Arab world."

"This was something I never expected in my life," Nonoo said, "to be ambassador in the United States. I think I've made a big impact on a lot of people, being female and representing Bahrain in the most important country in the world." Her reception by fellow Arab diplomats in Washington has been incredibly warm, she reported: "The Syrian ambassador recently hosted a dinner to honor me. The Iraqi ambassador had one . . . and Oman is having one. They've really made me feel at home."

On Yom Kippur, Nonoo attended Orthodox services. She may not, however, have any relationship with the Embassy of Israel, because Bahrain and Israel do not have diplomatic relations. "Understand that Israel and Judaism are two different things," she stated. "I've never felt any discrimination or anti-Semitism. My father was a very well-known figure. When he died in 1993 in a car accident, the amount of people who came to offer condolences—including the emir, the prime minister and the emir's other brother—was amazing. They all showed us respect."

Muslims and Jews Are Not Historic Enemies

The idea that there has been an ancient enmity between Jews and Muslims is completely ahistorical, and those Jewish groups and individuals who promote such a view seem to be unaware of the long history of cooperation between the two religions. Much has been written in recent years about the Golden Age of Jews in Muslim Spain. Indeed, when Muslim rule came to an end and the Catholic monarchs Ferdinand and Isabella expelled the Jews from Spain in 1492, they were welcomed into the Ottoman Empire. The anti-Semitism which plagued medieval Christian Europe was not to be found in the Islamic world.

In his recent book, *Among the Righteous*, Robert Satloff, who has served since 1993 as executive director of the Washington Institute for Near East Policy, unearths the lost stories of Arabs who saved Jews during the Holocaust. When the Nazis occupied the countries of North Africa and sought to round up Jews and expropriate Jewish property, Satloff notes, "in every place that it occurred, Arabs helped Jews. Some Arabs spoke out against the persecution of Jews and took public stands of unity with them. Some Arabs denied the support and assistance that would have made the wheels of the anti-Jewish campaign spin more efficiently.... And there were occasions when certain Arabs chose to do more than just offer moral support to Jews. They bravely saved Jewish lives, at times risking their own in the process. Those Arabs were true heroes."

"The idea that there has been an ancient enmity between Jews and Muslims is completely ahistorical."

Nor was it only in North Africa that Muslims saved Jews. During the Nazi occupation, the Grand Mosque of Paris provided sanctuary for Jews hiding from German and Vichy troops, and provided certificates of Muslim identity to untold numbers of Jews. Satloff quotes reports describing the mosque "as a virtual Grand Central Station for the Underground Railroad of Jews in France." This story is told in a 1991 film *Une Résistance Oubliée: La Mosquée de Paris* (*A Forgotten Resistance: The Mosque of Paris*) by Derri Berkani, a French documentary filmmaker of Algerian Berber origin.

The time has come to understand the real history of Jewish-Muslim relations—and those who are leading efforts to achieve mutual understanding between the two faiths are showing the way in this effort. The Palestinian-Israeli conflict is political and should not be confused with religion. Perhaps the day will come when Israel helps make that eminently clear by appointing as ambassador to the U.S. one of its own Muslim citizens.

Atheism Is Growing in the United States

Andrew Sullivan

In the following viewpoint, Andrew Sullivan reports on a 2009 survey of religious identification in the United States that demonstrates that an increasing number of Americans claim to be nonreligious and/or atheist. Sullivan argues that sex abuse scandals in the Catholic Church have led many former Catholics to abandon faith altogether. He further asserts that many former Christians are not identifying themselves as such because of the extreme political agenda set by evangelical Christians. He concludes that atheism will continue to grow until American Christianity demonstrates "intellectual responsibility." Sullivan is a columnist for the Sunday Times *in London.*

As you read, consider the following questions:

1. What percentage of the U.S. population claims to be atheist, according to Andrew Sullivan?
2. According to Sullivan, by how much has the number of Americans attending "megachurches" increased in the last twenty years?
3. Who are four people Sullivan cites as examples of serious American Christians from the past?

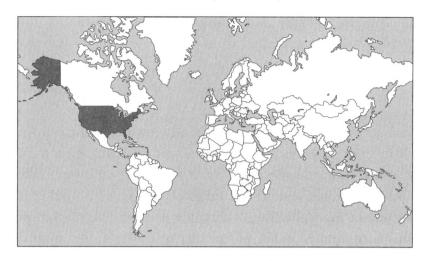

There is one thing that is not allowed in American national politics—and that is atheism. "In God We Trust" is on the currency; and the number of congressional members who avow no faith at all are about as plentiful as those who are openly gay (none in the Senate; five in the House).

Under the last president [George W. Bush], religious faith—evangelical Christianity or Benedict-style Catholicism—was a prerequisite for real access to the inner circle. But the requirement is not just Republican. Among the more excruciating campaign events of last year was a faith summit for the Democrats in which candidates vied with one another to express the most piety. Barack Obama's Christianity—educated, nuanced, social—is in many ways more striking than that of, say, [Richard] Nixon, [Harry] Truman or [Dwight D.] Eisenhower.

Americans Are Losing Faith

Americans are losing faith, though; and those who have it are moving out of established churches. The nonreligious are now the third biggest grouping in the US, after Catholics and Baptists, according to the just-released [2009] American Religious

Identification Survey. The bulk of this shift occurred in the 1990s, when they jumped from 8% to 14% of the population—but they have consolidated in the past decade to 15%.

As elsewhere in the West, mainline Protestantism has had the biggest drop—from 19% to 13%. Despite heavy Latino immigration, the proportion of Catholics has drifted down since 1990, and their numbers have shifted dramatically from the northeast and the rust belt to the south and west. Take South Carolina, a state you might associate with hard-core Protestant Evangelicalism. It certainly does exist there—but in that southern state, the percentage of Catholics has almost doubled since 1990 and the percentage of atheists has tripled.

"The nonreligious are now the third biggest grouping in the US, after Catholics and Baptists."

America, it turns out, is a more complicated spiritual place than the stereotypes might imply. Islam is still tiny—and integrated and largely successful. Catholicism, while buoyant among new Hispanic immigrants (who are, nonetheless, drifting rapidly towards Evangelicalism in the Southern Hemisphere whence they came), has plummeted in its heartland. Think of Massachusetts, the home of the Irish and Italian and Portuguese. In 1990, Catholics accounted for 54% of all residents of the Kennedys' state. That's now 39%.

The bulk of these ex-Catholics joined no other faith group—and the number of residents claiming no religion at all jumped from 8% to 22%. Of course, the sex abuse scandal played a powerful part. One of the chief enablers and protectors of abusive priests, Cardinal Bernard Law, was based in Boston and escaped real accountability by being given a prestigious sinecure in Rome. The Irish and Italians in Massachusetts did not forget.

A Snapshot of American Religious Identity: 2008

- 86% of Americans identified as Christians in 1990 and 76% in 2008.

- Mainline Protestant churches such as Episcopal, Presbyterian, Methodist, and Lutheran as well as the Catholic Church show the steepest decline in membership.

- One out of five Americans failed to indicate a religious identity in a 2008 survey.

- Asian Americans indicate no religious identity in greater numbers than do other racial or ethnic groups.

- 27% of Americans do not expect to have a religious funeral.

Barry A. Kosmin and Ariela Keysar,
American Religious Identification Survey (ARIS) 2008.

Politicized Evangelicals Versus Atheists

In many ways the most interesting dynamic is that between mega-church, politicised Evangelicalism and atheism. Mega-churches have emerged in many suburban neighbourhoods in America and serve as community centres, as social-work hubs and as venues for what most outsiders would think of as stadium-style Sunday rock shows, in which religion looks like a form of fandom. Charismatic preachers—like the now disgraced Ted Haggard [who resigned or was removed in 2006 following a sex scandal] or the politically powerful Rick Warren—have built massive congregations.

The movement has spawned its own shadow pop music industry, co-opts the popular culture as any brand-conscious franchise would and has a completely informal form of worship. Go to one of these places and it feels like a town in itself—with shops, daycare centres, conference rooms and social networking groups. The car parks feel like those in sports stadiums; and the atmosphere evokes a big match. In 20 years, the number of Americans finding identity and God in these places has soared from 200,000 to more than 8m [million].

Atheism as a Reaction to Evangelicalism

This is not, one hastens to add, an intellectual form of faith. It is a highly emotional and spontaneous variety of American Protestantism and theologically a blend of self-help, biblical literalism and Republican politics. This is, in many ways, how George W. Bush reframed conservatism in America—and with one in three Americans now calling themselves evangelical, you can see the political temptation. The problem was that the issues the evangelicals focused obsessively on—abortion, gays, stem cells, feeding tubes for those in permanent vegetative states—often came to seem warped to many others. Those who might once have passively called themselves Christian suddenly found the label toxic, if it meant identifying with such a specific political agenda. And so as Evangelicalism rose, atheism and nonaffiliation emerged as a reaction.

It is impossible to know where this is heading, but the latest survey is a reminder to exercise a little scepticism when you hear of America's religious exceptionalism. Yes, America is far more devout than most of western Europe; but it is not immune to the broader crises facing established religion in the West. The days when America's leading intellectuals contained a strong cadre of serious Christians are over. There is no Thomas Merton [Catholic writer and monk] in our day; no [American Protestant theologian] Reinhold Niebuhr, [Catholic author] Walker Percy or [Catholic author] Flannery O'Connor. In the arguments spawned by the new atheist wave, the Christian respondents have been underwhelming. As one evangelical noted in the *Christian Science Monitor* last week, "being against gay marriage and being rhetorically pro-life will not make up for the fact that massive majorities of evangelicals can't articulate the Gospel with any coherence".

"Those who might once have passively called themselves Christian suddenly found the label toxic, if it meant identifying with a specific political agenda."

The quality of the Catholic priesthood has also drifted downward: The next generation of priests is more orthodox, but also more insular and less engaged with the wider world. There are a few exceptions: The 29-year-old orthodox Catholic Ross Douthat has just won a treasured opinion column slot in the *New York Times*. But he is sadly an exception that proves a more general rule. American Christianity may be stronger in some pockets, but it is dumber, too. In the end, in the free marketplace of ideas and beliefs, that will count.

What one yearns for is a resuscitation of a via media [middle way] in American religious life—the role that the established Protestant churches once played. Or at least an understanding that religion must absorb and explain the new facts of modernity: the deepening of the Darwinian consensus in the sciences, the irrefutable scriptural scholarship that makes biblical literalism intellectually contemptible, the shifting shape of family life, the new reality of openly gay people, the fact of gender equality in the secular world. It seems to me that American Christianity, despite so many resources, has ignored its intellectual responsibility. And atheists, if this continues much longer, will continue to pick up that slack.

In Latin America, Established Religions and Sects Threaten Indigenous Cultures

Diego Cevallos

In the following viewpoint, Diego Cevallos argues that both established religions such as Catholicism and sects of evangelical Protestants are endangering the well-being of indigenous peoples in Latin America. He asserts that because many of the religious groups focus on political and social changes, they attempt to manipulate indigenous peoples to their causes. He adds that many of the sects require adherents to have beliefs that destroy cultural traditions. Cevallos is a writer specializing in indigenous issues for Inter Press Service.

As you read, consider the following questions:

1. How many Tzotzil Mayans have been killed because of religious conflicts in Mexico over the past thirty years?
2. Which Latin American countries have the largest indigenous populations?
3. What are critics referring to when they use the word "sects"?

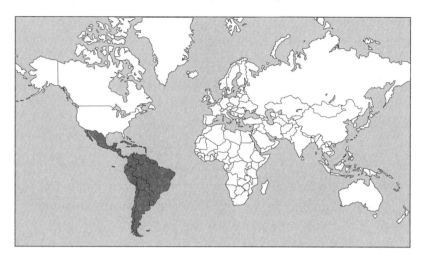

Indigenous communities throughout Latin America are facing the loss of their cultural traditions, divisive conflicts, and in some cases even bloodshed, all in the name of God.

Many of the frictions stem from the hundreds of religions and sects that have taken root in these communities, ranging from large, established denominations like the Roman Catholic, Lutheran, Adventist, Baptist and Mormon to newer, lesser-known groups such as the Church of the Word, the Fountain of Life, Alpha Omega and the Guardians of the Holy Sepulchre.

"Whatever religion they try to inculcate us with, it will have an impact in spiritual terms, which is in a way our Achilles' heel, since most of us indigenous peoples approach life from a spiritual level," Luis Macas, a Saraguro Indian and president of the Confederation of Indigenous Nationalities of Ecuador, remarked to IPS [Inter Press Service].

Traditional Beliefs Were Annihilated

Among the 40 million indigenous people who live in Latin America today, the most prevalent religion is still Roman Catholicism, forcibly and often violently imposed by the European "conquerors" in the 15th and 16th centuries through the complete annihilation or partial assimilation of pre-Columbian religious beliefs and practices.

But over the years, other religions have come to compete for the "souls" of the region's aboriginal peoples, especially during the 20th century, in an often rocky coexistence with the Catholic Church.

"Among the 40 million indigenous people who live in Latin America today, the most prevalent religion is still Roman Catholicism, forcibly and often violently imposed by European 'conquerors' in the 15th and 16th centuries."

In the last 30 years, the Tzotzil Mayan indigenous community of Chamula in the southern Mexican state of Chiapas has been shaken by 100 deaths resulting from religious conflicts.

Another 30,000 community members have been expelled for professing Protestant beliefs and thus incurring the wrath of local authorities, who practice a particularly orthodox brand of Catholicism that rejects the reforms of the Second Vatican Council of the 1960s, which promoted greater openness to other religions.

Expulsion, imprisonment, physical beatings and the denial of educational and medical services are among the manifestations of the religious sectarianism that has emerged in recent years in large areas of the southern Mexican states of Chiapas, Oaxaca and Guerrero, where the majority of the population is indigenous.

Politics and Religion

In Ecuador, a powerful and organised indigenous movement capable of leading massive social protests, overthrowing presidents and reaching government leadership positions earlier in the decade is now fragmented, and some observers say it is because one sector, allied with Protestant religions, continued to support President Lucio Gutiérrez, who was removed from office by Congress in late April [2005] after over a week of street protests.

In Guatemala and Bolivia, which along with Mexico, Ecuador and Peru are the Latin American countries with the largest indigenous populations, divisions have also been wrought by differences of religious affiliation, which often merges with support for particular political parties and local authorities.

"Many religions have destroyed what we are, and it is sad to see the contempt that the new generations have for what we once were."

"There are clearly internal problems in our communities provoked by religion, because some churches address social concerns, while others merely focus on spiritual matters and foster conformity, which has an obvious impact on the struggles of the indigenous people," noted Rafael González Yoc, spokesman for the Campesino Unity Committee (CUC) in Guatemala.

"Many religions have destroyed what we are, and it is sad to see the contempt that the new generations have for what we once were. They think that the traditional beliefs of the Mayans (the main indigenous ethnic group in Central America) are witchcraft, or satanic," he commented to IPS.

According to González Yoc, the Church of the Word and Assembly of God, both of which are evangelical Protestant denominations based in the United States, were implanted in indigenous communities in Guatemala to collaborate with the military dictatorships of the 1970s and 1980s.

Sociologist and journalist Roger Pascual of the Spanish nongovernmental group Agencia de Información Solidaria maintains that these two churches were backed by the U.S. government to combat anything that appeared somehow linked to communism in Guatemala.

Liberation Theology

It was during this same period that the Liberation Theology movement within the Catholic Church had come to exercise a major influence in Central America.

Liberation Theology is based on a "preferential option for the poor", and its proponents' involvement in the struggles of the poor and marginalised sectors of the population gave them common cause with the leftist revolutionary movements active in the region at the time. As a result, the Catholic Church came to be viewed by some as a dangerously "Marxist" institution.

In his "Analysis of the Incursion of Sects into the Political Spheres of Latin America", Pascual states, "The U.S. government contributed to building up the Assembly of God Pentecostal sect to such an extent that it came to control 1,500 houses of worship, in addition to numerous television and radio stations" in Guatemala.

In addition, he notes, "The (Ronald) Reagan administration (1981–1989) was also behind the establishment of the Church of the Word, which collaborated in the coup d'état led by General José Efraín Ríos Montt in 1982."

Guatemala was engulfed in a civil war from 1960 until 1996. Of the roughly 200,000 people who were killed (including 45,000 "disappeared") by the government security forces, the majority were Mayan Indians. The war also led to the internal displacement of one million people and the exodus of 500,000 refugees to Mexico alone, while 250,000 children were orphaned.

"Religions have an impact on our collective behaviour, and change the essence of the way in which we are organised in communities and families. Because of religion, the traditionally collective nature of indigenous peoples has given way to individualism, and is dividing us," said Macas.

The Pope Claims That Catholicism Is Good for Indigenous Peoples

During his [2007] trip to Latin America, Pope Benedict XVI offended millions when he arrogantly suggested that Catholicism had purified indigenous populations, and called the resurgence of indigenous religions a step backward. He also said the native populations were longing for Christianity and had welcomed the Catholic priests at the time of European conquest.

He tried to clean it up afterwards by noting the "sufferings and injustices inflicted by the colonizers on the indigenous populations whose human and basic rights often were trampled," but the damage was done.

David A. Love,
"Pope Benedict Argues Catholic
Church 'Purified' Indigenous Peoples,"
AlterNet, June 18, 2007. www.alternet.org.

The Growth of Religious Sects

"There are a huge number of sects in Ecuador, I believe over 300, whose role is to pacify, divide and tame the people, subordinating them to the interests of the dominant powers or big corporations, like the oil companies," he added.

When critics talk about "sects," they are referring to more recently founded Protestant denominations and churches, as opposed to established religions like the Baptist, Episcopalian, Lutheran or Presbyterian churches.

The Roman Catholic hierarchy, together with some anthropologists and civil society organisations, accuse these new sects of recruiting indigenous followers with money and the offer of "salvation," while promoting beliefs that break with their cultural traditions and way of life.

Some Catholic leaders have used highly confrontational language in referring to these upstart Protestant churches. "You have to be shameless to be a Protestant," declared the cardinal of Guadalajara, Mexico, Juan Sandoval Iñiguez, while the former papal nuncio to Mexico, Girolamo Prigione, commented that "these sects are like flies that ought to be swatted with a newspaper."

Mexican writer Carlos Monsiváis has criticised this Catholic religious intolerance, claiming that it breeds persecution and denies indigenous people the right to change their beliefs, as if Catholicism were the only religion that should be practised in these communities, an attitude he calls "absurd".

But many critics of these new Protestant denominations, including followers of Liberation Theology—who have a long tradition of demanding respect for the rights of indigenous peoples and fighting against the oppression they suffer—believe that they distort the message of God, and in some cases merely serve to foster ideological control by the United States.

"These sects create individuals who are mindless and alienated. They kill the soul of the people," said Spanish-born Bishop Pedro Casaldáliga, a leading exponent of Liberation Theology who devoted almost 40 years of his life to working with the poor in Brazil.

For his part, Pope John Paul II issued a number of documents and declarations condemning these sects during his 1978–2005 papacy, while he promoted dialogue with established Protestant churches, Judaism and Islam.

Sects that use healing, exorcism and promises of prosperity to attract followers are "a danger to Christians" and should be condemned in the same way as drug trafficking and birth control campaigns, the late pope stated during a visit to Brazil in 1991.

One denomination in particular, the U.S.-based Jehovah's Witnesses, has clashed with authorities in the region because of the fact that its members refuse to pay tribute to national flags and other patriotic symbols. They also cannot give blood or receive transfusions.

Eugenio Poma, a Bolivian Aymara Indian, Methodist bishop and coordinator of the Indigenous Pastoral Committee of the Latin American Council of Churches (CLAI), which represents over 150 established denominations, told IPS that these new religious groups "that are growing like mushrooms" respond to "dark" interests.

"There are churches that only pursue spiritual indoctrination, like many of these sects, and then there are others among us who go into communities to learn and to help. Obviously, we are guided by very different interests, and this separates us," said Poma.

Nevertheless, he added, the "indigenous heart, which strives for a life as part of a community and fights for its rights" will eventually prevail.

"In the end we will struggle together, even though we belong to different faiths. I believe we should come together and listen to each other, because when it comes down to it, all of us indigenous peoples want the same thing," he concluded.

Periodical Bibliography

The following articles have been selected to supplement the diverse views presented in this chapter.

Gary Bauer — "What Are U.S. Students Learning About Islam? Politically Correct Textbooks Are Distorting Key Concepts and Historical Facts," *Christian Science Monitor*, April 22, 2009.

Preeti Bhattacharji — "Backgrounder: Religion in China, Council on Foreign Relations," May 16, 2008. www.cfr.org.

Economist — "Of Saints and Sinners: Sufism," December 20, 2008.

Barry A. Kosmin and Ariela Keysar — "Summary Report: American Religious Identification Survey (ARIS 2008)," 2009. www.americanreligionsurvey-aris.org.

New African — "Africans Became Christians Long Before Europeans," October 2008.

Peter C. Phan — "Praying to the Buddha: Living Amid Religious Pluralism," *Commonweal*, vol. 134, no. 2, January 26, 2007. www.commonwealmagazine.org.

V.V. Raman — "Religious Tolerance in a Pluralistic World," *Tikkun*, vol. 23, no. 6, November–December 2008.

Emma Terama — "Religious Fundamentalism and Secularism on the Increase," *Signtific*, January 8, 2008. www.signtific.org.

Vanguard — "Nigeria: The Power of Fiction—A Philosophical Critique of Religion," July 20, 2008.

Robin Wright — "Islam's Soft Revolution," *TIME*, vol. 173, no. 12, March 30, 2009.

Religion, Science, and Education

Europe Supports Secular Education

Roy W. Brown

In the following excerpt from a speech delivered at a European Parliament seminar, Roy W. Brown argues that European education is being threatened by attacks from those who want creationism and/or intelligent design taught in schools. He asserts that Europe must remain secular to guarantee freedom of religion for all citizens. He also argues that creationism is a political and religious construct that should not be substituted for science. Schools, Brown asserts, must not be a site for religious indoctrination. Brown is the former president of the International Humanist and Ethical Union.

As you read, consider the following questions:

1. What are the two sides in the political struggle over the teaching of creationism, according to Roy W. Brown?

2. What was the pope's response to the Berlin Declaration, according to Brown?

3. What does Brown argue will be the outcome if Europe accepts a special status for any religious belief?

Evolution happens. The *Theory* of Evolution is not about *whether* evolution happens but about *how* it happens. But what we are faced with now in Europe is an extension of what

Roy W. Brown, "The Politics of Values: The Brussels Declaration and Its Political Importance," International Humanist and Ethical Union, April 17, 2007. Reproduced by permission of the author.

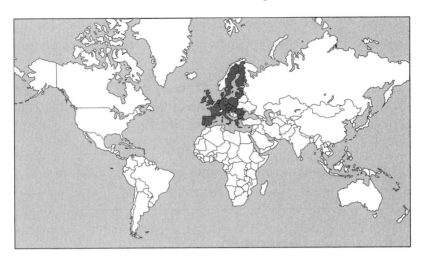

we have already seen in America and in many other parts of the world: the demonising of science, and attempts to replace science by pseudo-science in the classroom.

The promotion of the teaching of creationism or so-called "intelligent design" as part of the science curriculum is part of a far wider agenda. It is part of a political struggle between, on the one hand, an authoritarian attempt to promote particular religions at all costs, and on the other hand, a desire to uphold the secular principles and values of the European Enlightenment. . . .

The Importance of Secularism

Secularism has recently come under sustained attack in Europe. It has been misrepresented as equivalent to atheism, as anti-religious, and as wanting to banish religion from the public square. This is totally misleading. Secularism is not the same thing as militant atheism. It does not imply that religious believers and their leaders should be silenced, but it does imply that no particular belief should have a privileged position or privileged access to the institutions of government. Secularism means *neutrality* in matters of religion and belief: It favours none and discriminates against none. Secularism is, in fact, the *only* guarantee of freedom of religion or belief for every citizen.

It is vital that Europe defend its secular heritage and the values of democracy, equality, individual freedom and the rule of law—the values on which our civilisation is based.

"Secularism is, in fact, the only *guarantee of freedom of religion or belief for every citizen."*

The Brussels Declaration

Six weeks ago [March 2007], here in the European Parliament, we [Members of the European Parliament, Catholics for a Free Choice, the International Humanist and Ethical Union, the European Humanist Federation, and the European Parliament Working Group on the Separation of Religion and Politics] launched the Brussels Declaration, a restatement of the common values that underpin our civilisation. The declaration has now been signed by thousands of ordinary European citizens as well as by nearly 1000 distinguished European leaders, including eminent scientists, academics, journalists, writers, religious and community leaders, several Nobel laureates, and politicians from across the political spectrum and throughout Europe, including over 80 members of the European Parliament. We launched the Brussels Declaration in the context of the lead-up to the 50th anniversary of the Treaty of Rome [1957 treaty that established the European Economic Community] and of reported plans to publish a Berlin Declaration as a prelude to opening negotiations for a new Constitutional Treaty for Europe.

It was reported that these plans would "bring God back into the Constitution", not simply by paying lip service in the preamble to Europe's supposed Judeo-Christian heritage, but by providing special access for religious leaders to promote

A Secular Vision for Europe: State Neutrality

No religion or belief should suffer discrimination compared to any other, nor should any religion or belief be especially privileged, for to privilege one is to discriminate against all others.

State neutrality in matters of religion is the only means by which the rights of all, believers and non-believers alike, can be protected. The neutrality of the state therefore needs to be constitutionally guaranteed.

State neutrality does not free religious groups from their obligation to abide by the law. Incitement to violence for example, cannot be permitted on the grounds of religious freedom.

Those who seek to reintroduce religious privilege into public life frequently but wrongly equate the secular state with an atheist state, but secularism is not atheism. The secular state is neutral in matters of religion and belief, favouring none and discriminating against none. Only the secular state can guarantee the equal treatment of all citizens.

Democrats, of whatever religious persuasion, have fought to defend the secular state. Many religious are among the most stalwart defenders of secularism because they understand the danger of allowing religious privilege and discrimination to enter government and public life.

Committee for a Vision for Europe, Brussels,
"A Secular Vision for Europe," March 25, 2007. www.iheu.org.

their views within the institutions of the European Union. Such an outcome would be anti-democratic. All European citizens already have equal rights to express their views through the ballot box and via the media, including the Internet. All can participate in the marketplace of ideas. Additional privileged access for certain persons, however respected and eminent, could undermine the democratic process.

Europe's Values Are Not Exclusively Religious

In the event, the final text of the Berlin Declaration was secular, with no mention of gods or religion. Some religious leaders were severely disappointed. The pope spoke of "Europe's apostasy" and of "Europe abandoning its values". But Europe's values are not exclusively religious, nor are they those of a single religion. Europe as a whole has not agreed on a single set of religious values for centuries, as we know to our cost from the wars in which religious differences have played a part. Nor do we need any special constitutional provisions for religion. Absolute freedom of religion or belief is already guaranteed by the European Convention on Human Rights and Fundamental Freedoms.

The Brussels Declaration is a declaration of universal values, not those of a single religion or culture. Many religious institutions remain uncomfortable about some aspects of democracy and human rights. Some reject equality of the sexes, and some seem irremediably homophobic. Furthermore, religious leaders, whatever their claims, do not necessarily speak for all the believers of their faith. Why then should their opinions be given precedence over those of the people of Europe, or indeed any special consideration at all? Those who follow Islamic, Hindu, Buddhist, Catholic, Orthodox, Protestant or any other religious teachings are free to do so in their own lives and are even free to proselytise. But they should not be permitted, much less encouraged, to impose their views on others. No religion should be permitted to interfere in the private lives of others.

Which brings us to back to education. In the Brussels Declaration we affirm the right of everyone to an open and comprehensive education. Education should be about teaching children to think and to find answers for themselves. Schools should not be used for indoctrination.

Certainly, parents have the right to impart their own values and religious beliefs to their children, but states have no obligation to support them in doing so. States do, however, have a responsibility to provide information and education *about* all religions and widely held beliefs. Teaching that one religion is true and all others are false, or that one religion provides the only acceptable source of values, or presenting religious beliefs as science, is not education, but indoctrination.

"Teaching that one religion is true and all others are false, or that one religion provides the only acceptable source of values, or presenting religious beliefs as science, is not education, but indoctrination."

We are engaged in a war of values: a war for the soul of Europe. If we accept special status for any belief, we shall be setting the stage for conflict for generations to come. We need a society that respects the human rights of all, and that does not seek to restrict them in the name of religion. Our values are well expressed in the Brussels Declaration.

Scottish Students Study Religion

Andrew Collier

In the following viewpoint, Andrew Collier argues that Scottish students are studying religion in growing numbers. He suggests several reasons for this trend including the fact that religion is an inherently interesting subject, religion is an important part of the Scottish culture and history, and that although religion is currently under attack, it survives best when scrutinized. He also asserts that students study both religion and science and that they are not mutually exclusive, but rather are supportive of each other. Collier is a Scottish journalist.

As you read, consider the following questions:

1. According to Andrew Collier, on what are Western standards of morality based?
2. According to Collier, what do secularists call religion?
3. Who argues the case for God, according to Collier?

In the dim and distant days when I was at school, God wasn't someone who engaged me very much. I can remember virtually nothing of my five years of religious education classes, save that I once got into trouble for chalking rude words on the teacher's door.

Andrew Collier, "So Why Have God Lessons Suddenly Hit a Higher Level?" *Daily Mail*, August 15, 2007, p. 12. Copyright © 2007 Solo Syndication Limited. Reproduced by permission.

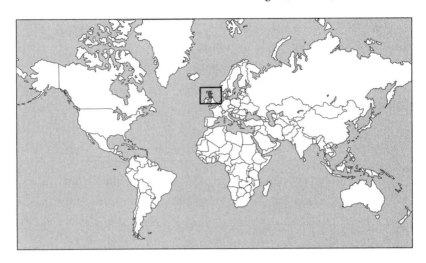

My mates and I saw religion as being the preserve of either the odd, brainy, wimpish kids in sandals who didn't want to be sullied by our heathen company, or the few Roman Catholics who managed to get a much-envied opt-out from the numbing dreariness of RE [religious education]. In short, we didn't do God.

Today's youngsters, though, are much more likely to be interested in what He has to offer. New figures released this week [August 2007] show that religious education in Scottish schools is now decidedly in fashion, with the number of pupils taking the subject at Higher Grade having increased by a third since last year.

On the face of it, this seems bizarre.

Students See Religion as Worthy of Study

After all, attendance at Scottish churches remains in steady decline, with youngsters particularly absent from the pews. The answer to this conundrum is probably that today's pupils have yet to be convinced of the merits of attending mainstream worship, but they see religion as a subject fascinating in itself and worthy of serious study.

Of course, they are right about it being a gripping classroom subject. Religion is arguably the most intellectually challenging and interesting of academic disciplines.

It is a fascinating and complex amalgam of other elements—philosophy, history, geography, theology, science and art.

"New figures released . . . [in August 2007] show that religious education in Scottish schools is now decidedly in fashion, with the number of pupils taking the subject at Higher Grade having increased by a third since . . . [2006]."

Religion can mean studying the origins of the universe, the beauty and wisdom of the Psalms, the arguments of the Buddha or Plato, the politics of the Victorian era or the paintings of Michelangelo or Giotto—and that's just for starters. An easy option? Come off it. A single term's study of this stuff has more meat in it than an entire degree course in soft lifestyle subjects such as media studies.

Religion and Scottish History

In Scotland, religion simply cannot be separated from our history as a nation.

That's one of the reasons it's so fascinating and appealing to school pupils. The country's fundamental character has been shaped by Celtic Christianity, the Reformation, the Kirk [Church of Scotland] and the 19th century rebirth of Roman Catholicism.

Western standards of morality are still based on the Ten Commandments and the Sermon on the Mount. Even today, whether it's the Church of Scotland sounding off against Trident [British nuclear weapons] or Cardinal Keith O'Brien [the head of the Scottish Catholic Church] campaigning against abortion, Christianity touches our lives on an almost daily basis.

But religion is about far more than Christianity, and the Higher course—its full title is Religious, Moral and Philosophical Studies—recognises this.

Modern Scotland is an inclusive, multicultural society with modern faith communities living in relative harmony: How we maintain and strengthen that inclusivity against a background of global jihad and growing Christian fundamentalism is arguably the greatest challenge facing us today.

The recent [June 2007] bombing of Glasgow Airport and the death of Scottish soldiers in Iraq and Afghanistan provide powerful evidence of the fact that religion is not confined to dusty textbooks or scrolls in Dead Sea caves. It is of central importance to us all, here and now.

As well as its relevance, there's another good reason why religious education in schools is so popular.

Religion Performs Well When Under Attack

At present, religion in general and Christianity in particular . . . [are] under attack as never before.

Secularists dismiss it as superstitious mumbo jumbo.

Leftwing politicians try to marginalise it in favour of their trendy, morally bankrupt causes. Extreme American evangelists such as Pat Robertson and Fred Phelps reduce it to ridicule.

Yet history has shown that religion performs at its best when it is under pressure. It also has astonishing longevity.

Atheistic belief systems such as Nazism, communism and Marxism have come and gone in a few decades: The church has survived for 2,000 years, Islam for 1,500 and Buddhism and Hinduism longer than both.

Religion in Scotland: A Snapshot

	Number (in thousands)	Percentage (%)
Church of Scotland	2,146.3	42.40
Roman Catholic	803.7	15.88
Other Christian	344.6	6.81
Buddhist	6.8	0.13
Hindu	5.6	0.11
Jewish	6.4	0.13
Muslim	42.6	0.84
Sikh	6.6	0.13
Another religion	27.0	0.53
All religions	**3,389.5**	**66.96**
No religion	1,394.5	27.55
Not answered	278.1	5.49
All no religion/not answered	**1,672.5**	**33.04**
Base	5,062.0	100.00

TAKEN FROM: "Analysis of Religion in 2001 Census," The Scottish Government, 2005. www.scotland.gov.uk.

As has happened so many times before, the knives are currently out for God. We are seeing the growth of a new and revitalised assault by atheists who attempt to intellectualise the case against religion. Chief among these new secularists is Richard Dawkins, whose work *The God Delusion* has proved to be one of the unlikeliest best sellers of the decade.

Dawkins, an evolutionary biologist, has produced a work in which some of the arguments are plausible, but others astonishingly lacklustre. The existence of God, he concludes, is a scientific question. Well, it would be, wouldn't it?

I don't agree with Dawkins but I do welcome his book, because I think it has had precisely the opposite effect to that intended. By castigating religion, he has acted as a Trojan horse for it.

His hypotheses, and those of other modern atheists like him, are clearly stimulating young, enquiring minds in Scottish schools and elsewhere.

For every Dawkins, there is a Hans Küng [a Catholic theologian], a C.S. Lewis [twentieth-century writer], a St. Thomas Aquinas arguing the case for God. The children themselves can work out who is right and take great pleasure and gain challenge in doing so.

Science and Religion

It is particularly encouraging that Scottish youngsters are studying religion and belief systems alongside science and technology.

Ever since the Enlightenment, in which Scotland's role was so profound, there has been an underlying assumption that science and God are mutually exclusive—if you believe in one, then it raises serious questions about the other.

"It is particularly encouraging that Scottish youngsters are studying religion and belief systems alongside science and technology."

In fact, as an increasing number of people are coming to realise, the reverse is true.

When science flags, religion picks up the baton.

Take the theory of the Big Bang, for instance. Physicists can explain events up to about two billionths of a second before the explosion which created the universe, but they cannot explain the explosion itself. This leaves open the possibility of it being triggered by a single supreme creator.

After the bang, as we all know, unimaginable quantities of material rushed out all over the cosmos. One would presume that the DNA which eventually led to human life on Earth would have been replicated many times over in this new, vastly dispersed universe.

By the laws of science, species identical or similar to man should be thriving on a million planets in a thousand galaxies.

Yet as far as we can tell, mankind is unique. If this isn't intelligent God-inspired design, what is?

There are other areas in which science and religion come together. There is an interesting test which physicists can carry out—the double-slit experiment—which appears to prove an atom can be in two places at once. In other words, it seems to be evidence of a parallel universe. Heaven, perhaps?

Religion Is Relevant

This all goes to prove that religion, far from being some sort of lost cause for spiritual anoraks, is supremely and wonderfully relevant to the way we live now. It is more than churches and mosques, more than crescents and crucifixes, more even than jihad or Judaism. It is alive and kicking, with God and all His astonishing works at the heart of everything we see, hear and do.

"[Religion] is alive and kicking, with God and all His astonishing works at the heart of everything we see, hear and do."

It's all very well to worship the Lord in the beauty of holiness, but there is a lot more to religion than that. One can only be inspired that our youngsters are bold and adventurous enough to help absorb—and perhaps in later years, push—the frontiers of understanding in what surely must be mankind's greatest intellectual quest of all.

American Researchers Believe Religion Is an Evolutionary Asset

The Independent

In the following viewpoint, the writers from the Independent *describe American research into the biological origins of religion. Although not all researchers are in agreement that religion has a biological basis, many researchers suggest that religion is an evolutionary development that has increased the chances of survival of the species. Scientists have not located a particular part of the brain responsible for religious feelings but argue that religious belief is embedded deeply in several areas of the brain. The* Independent *is a British newspaper.*

As you read, consider the following questions:

1. In what journal was the latest study involving brain analysis of volunteers asked to think about religious and moral problems?
2. What do temporal-lobe epileptics suffering seizures frequently report, according to the viewpoint?
3. Why did researchers from the University of Pennsylvania inject radioactive isotopes into the brains of Buddhists in meditation, and what did they find out?

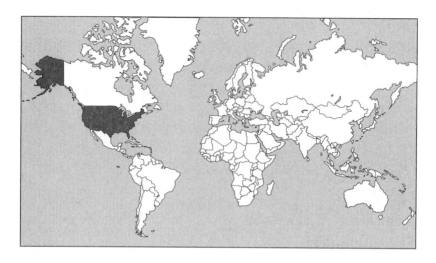

A belief in God is deeply embedded in the human brain, which is programmed for religious experiences, according to a study that analyses why religion is a universal human feature that has encompassed all cultures throughout history.

Scientists searching for the neural "God spot," which is supposed to control religious belief, believe that there is not just one but several areas of the brain that form the biological foundations of religious belief.

The researchers said their findings support the idea that the brain has evolved to be sensitive to any form of belief that improves the chances of survival, which could explain why a belief in God and the supernatural became so widespread in human evolutionary history.

"Scientists searching for the neural 'God spot,' which is supposed to control religious belief, believe that there is not just one but several areas of the brain that form the biological foundations of religious belief."

"Religious belief and behaviour are a hallmark of human life, with no accepted animal equivalent, and found in all cultures," said Professor Jordan Grafman, from the US National

Institute of Neurological Disorders and Stroke in Bethesda, near Washington, D.C. "Our results are unique in demonstrating that specific components of religious belief are mediated by well-known brain networks, and they support contemporary psychological theories that ground religious belief within evolutionary-adaptive cognitive functions."

Scientists are divided on whether religious belief has a biological basis. Some evolutionary theorists have suggested that Darwinian natural selection may have put a premium on individuals if they were able to use religious belief to survive hardships that may have overwhelmed those with no religious convictions. Others have suggested that religious belief is a side effect of a wider trait in the human brain to search for coherent beliefs about the outside world. Religion and the belief in God, they argue, are just a manifestation of this intrinsic, biological phenomenon that makes the human brain so intelligent and adaptable.

The latest study, published in the journal *Proceedings of the National Academy of Sciences*, involved analysing the brains of volunteers, who had been asked to think about religious and moral problems and questions. For the analysis, the researchers used a functional magnetic-resonance imaging machine, which can identify the most energetically-active regions of the brain.

They found that people of different religious persuasions and beliefs, as well as atheists, all tended to use the same electrical circuits in the brain to solve a perceived moral conundrum—and the same circuits were used when religiously-inclined people dealt with issues related to God.

The study found that several areas of the brain are involved in religious belief, one within the frontal lobes of the cortex—which are unique to humans—and another in the more evolutionary-ancient regions deeper inside the brain, which humans share with apes and other primates, Professor Grafman said.

Religion Helped Societies Survive

[Researcher Joseph Bulbulia] agrees that religious belief probably had a role in human evolution because it has helped societies survive and thrive for thousands of years.

Without religion, Bulbulia says, "large scale cooperation, which now spans the world, would be impossible." He adds that humans differ from other species in their ability to cooperate in very large groups.

Religion can help foster cooperation because it ensures that people share the same set of rules about behavior.

Jon Hamilton,
"To the Brain, God Is Just Another Guy,"
NPR Radio, March 9, 2009. www.npr.org.

"There is nothing unique about religious belief in these brain structures. Religion doesn't have a 'God spot' as such, instead it's embedded in a whole range of other belief systems in the brain that we use every day," Professor Grafman said.

The search for the God spot has in the past led scientists to many different regions of the brain. An early contender was the brain's temporal lobe, a large section of the brain that sits over each ear, because temporal-lobe epileptics suffering seizures in these regions frequently report having intense religious experiences. One of the principal exponents of this idea was Vilayanur Ramachandran, from the University of California, San Diego, who asked several of his patients with temporal-lobe epilepsy to listen to a mixture of religious, sexual and neutral words while measuring their levels of arousal and emotional reactions. Religious words elicited an unusually high response in these patients.

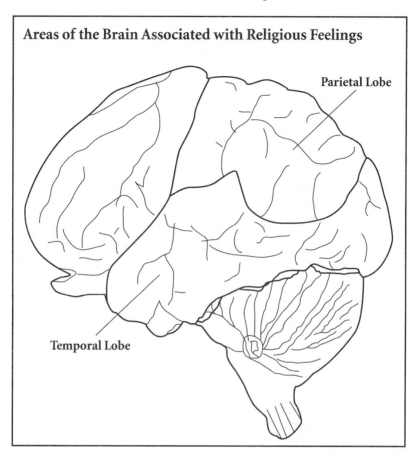

Areas of the Brain Associated with Religious Feelings

Parietal Lobe

Temporal Lobe

This work was followed by a study where scientists tried to stimulate the temporal lobes with a rotating magnetic field produced by a "God helmet". Michael Persinger, from Laurentian University in Ontario, found that he could artificially create the experience of religious feelings—the helmet's wearer reports being in the presence of a spirit or having a profound feeling of cosmic bliss.

Dr. Persinger said that about eight in every 10 volunteers report quasi-religious feelings when wearing his helmet. However, when Professor Richard Dawkins, an evolutionist and renowned atheist, wore it during the making of a BBC documentary, he famously failed to find God, saying that the helmet only affected his breathing and his limbs.

Other studies of people taking part in Buddhist meditation suggested the parietal lobes at the upper back region of the brain were involved in controlling religious belief, in particular the mystical elements that gave people a feeling of being on a higher plane during prayer.

"[A March 2009 study] suggests the brain is inherently sensitive to believing in almost anything if there are grounds for doing so, but when there is a mystery about something, the same neural machinery is co-opted in the formation of religious belief."

Andrew Newberg, from the University of Pennsylvania, injected radioactive isotope into Buddhists at the point at which they achieved meditative nirvana. Using a special camera, he captured the distribution of the tracer in the brain, which led the researchers to identify the parietal lobes as playing a key role during this transcendental state.

Professor Grafman was more interested in how people coped with everyday moral and religious questions. He said that the latest study, published today, suggests the brain is inherently sensitive to believing in almost anything if there are grounds for doing so, but when there is a mystery about something, the same neural machinery is co-opted in the formulation of religious belief.

"When we have incomplete knowledge of the world around us, it offers us the opportunities to believe in God. When we don't have a scientific explanation for something, we tend to rely on supernatural explanations," said Professor Grafman, who believes in God. "Maybe obeying supernatural forces that we had no knowledge of made it easier for religious forms of belief to emerge."

In Europe, Creationism Must Be Curbed

Peter C. Kjærgaard

In the following viewpoint, Peter C. Kjærgaard reports that creationism is infiltrating European culture and schools. The Council of Europe Parliamentary Assembly is worried about the development and urges member nations to support science. Kjærgaard notes that there is also a rise in Muslim and Christian creationism. One of the worst examples of this, according to the author, is the book Atlas of Creation *by Adnan Oktar (under the pseudonym Harun Yahya). Kjærgaard urges readers to take the threat posed by creationists seriously because it threatens academic knowledge. Kjærgaard is a professor at the University of Aarhus in Denmark.*

As you read, consider the following questions:

1. What resolution was passed on October 4, 2007, by the Council of Europe Parliamentary Assembly?
2. What did the Polish deputy minister of education tell the *Gazeta Wyborcza* (a Polish newspaper), according to Peter C. Kjærgaard?
3. In what year was the bicentenary of Charles Darwin's birth and the 150th anniversary of the publication of *On the Origin of Species?*

Peter C. Kjærgaard, "Western Front: While Secularists Sleep Well-Funded Creationists Are on the March in Europe," *New Humanist*, vol. 123, no. 3, May/June 2008. Copyright © 2008 The Rationalist Association. Reproduced by permission.

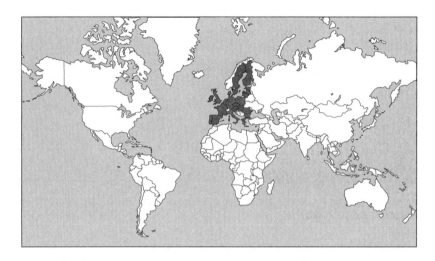

On 4 October 2007 the Council of Europe Parliamentary Assembly passed Resolution 1580, which issued a stark warning: Creationism, the denial of Darwinian evolution, is on the rise in Europe. The resolution focused on the way that creationists across the continent, using the model pioneered in America, have been targeting education, and warned of "a real risk of serious confusion being introduced into our children's minds between what has to do with convictions, beliefs, ideals of all sorts and what has to do with science". "An 'all things are equal' attitude," it concludes, "may seem appealing and tolerant, but is in fact dangerous."

The resolution urged member states to "defend and promote scientific knowledge" and "firmly oppose the teaching of creationism as a scientific discipline on an equal footing with the theory of evolution." But what provoked this European body to issue such an uncharacteristically clear and forthright statement?

The Rise of Creationism

The resolution was based on a comprehensive report prepared by the Committee on Culture, Science and Education and delivered to the assembly by the special rapporteur Guy Lengagne on 5 June 2007. This report synthesized research from across the EU citing examples of the rise of creationism in 14 member states, as well as significant non-members Russia, Serbia and Turkey. Examples cited of a growing creationist influence ranged from subtle downgrading of evolution in science education to outright attacks on the validity of Darwinism and the personality of Darwin himself. In Greece, the report found, evolution education was relegated to the very bottom of the science curriculum, which often meant in effect that secondary students learned nothing about it because of a lack of time. In Switzerland organisations like The European Biblical Centre and the ProGenesis group were devoting considerable resources to promoting creationist education. In Russia a 16-year-old girl launched a court case against the Ministry of Education, backed by the Russian Orthodox Church, challenging the teaching of just one "theory" of biology in school textbooks as a breach of her human rights. In the UK in 2006 the Intelligent Design propagandists Truth in Science sent out a "teaching pack" to every secondary school and sixth-form college in the country.

One of the more bizarre cases cited by the report comes from Poland, where in October 2006 deputy minister of education Miroslaw Orzechowski told the *Gazeta Wyborcza* that "the theory of evolution is a lie, an error that we have legalised as a common truth." He further argued that evolution is the "feeble idea of an aged non-believer" and put this error down to the fact that Darwin was "a vegetarian and lacked fire inside him".

Muslim Creationism

Each of these cases confirms the existence of a strong Christian creationist lobby in Europe, but the report also focused its attention on a new phenomenon—the rise of Muslim creationism. The central figure here is the Turkish Muslim creationist Adnan Oktar, who, writing under the pen name Harun

Yahya, has made a career out of attacking Darwinian evolution. Oktar is a figure fairly well-known to Darwinists and despite his claims to scientific competence is clearly little more than a crank. However, what had changed, according to the report, was the scale and ambition of Oktar's pseudo-scientific message. Since 2006 copies of a substantial, glossy and smartly packaged book called *Atlas of Creation*, credited to Harun Yahya, had been arriving at schools and universities across Europe. In Spain, France, Switzerland and Denmark clear evidence of the growing resources and confidence of European Muslim creationism was thudding on to the mat. The book is the first of a projected seven-part series, and parts two and three have already begun arriving at educational institutes Europe-wide.

Clearly, for the assembly, the report amounted to strong evidence that creationists were working strategically across Europe, with the aim of influencing the science curriculum as well as public opinion. Though it does not say so explicitly, the implication of the report is that creationists of different denominations and faiths are, or might soon be, working together in a concerted assault on science teaching, in the same way that American creationists have been for the past decade. In response to the call for action from the assembly, only the Swedish government acted promptly, swiftly issuing a general ban on the teaching of creationism and Intelligent Design in their schools.

"Each of these cases [sharing a rise in creationism] confirms the existence of a strong Christian creationist lobby in Europe."

My own copy of *Atlas of Creation*, all six kilos, arrived in 2006, just after my research group at the University of Aarhus had launched our Darwin in Denmark project, with online editions of Danish translations of Charles Darwin's writings. In fact 20 copies arrived, unrequested and completely free.

Hardbound and expensively produced with almost 800 pages of text and images printed on glossy paper, this book presents one of the most remarkable attacks not only on the theory of evolution but on science itself. The book is full of scientific jargon, diagrams and tables, and appears to discuss Darwinian evolution in detail and refute it through careful consideration of the evidence of the fossil record, animal biology and the history of science. Most of this is the same old tired creationism, emphasising the gaps in the fossil record and making much of the various scientific hoaxes like "Piltdown Man" which, it argues, were attempts by Darwinians to fabricate proof for their hypothesis.

Creationist Accuses Darwin of Great Evil

One of the most astonishing claims in the book is that Charles Darwin—the quiet Victorian gentleman naturalist—was responsible for the worst evils of the 20th century: racism, communism, fascism, Nazism, terrorism and, ultimately, 9/11. In a piece of overt symbolic theatre, the book's creators marked the anniversary of 9/11 last year by sending the *Atlas* to a large number of Protestant priests across Europe. The message was clear: In the fight against the theory of evolution, Christians and Muslims stand united.

"Just as manipulative as the worst of American creationists, European creationists are hard at work and some of them have a lot of money."

But despite the hyperbolic claims, the shock caused by *Atlas of Creation* is largely unrelated to its contents, which do not stand up to even the most cursory scrutiny. The real point is that before the book arrived many had no idea there was a resurgent Muslim creationism in Europe, and certainly didn't

Resolution 1580, Section 19: The Dangers of Creationism in Education

The Parliamentary Assembly [of the Council of Europe] ... urges the member states, and especially their education authorities to:

1. defend and promote scientific knowledge;

2. strengthen the teaching of the foundations of science, its history, its epistemology and its methods alongside the teaching of objective scientific knowledge;

3. make science more comprehensible, more attractive and closer to the realities of the contemporary world;

4. firmly oppose the teaching of creationism as a scientific discipline on an equal footing with the theory of evolution and in general the presentation of creationist ideas in any discipline other than religion;

5. promote the teaching of evolution as a fundamental scientific theory in the school curriculums.

Resolution 1580 (2007): The Dangers of Creationism in Education, Parliamentary Assembly, Council of Europe, October 4, 2007.

know it was so well-funded and organised. Who, people began to ask, is bankrolling Oktar's Science Research Foundation or Global Publishing of Istanbul, which published and distributed the book? So far no one has been able to find out, and all Oktar says is that he is funded by donations.

Creationism Is a Danger to Europe

One thing is clear: Creationism has indeed come to Europe and unfortunately, therefore, we have to take it seriously. We can't afford to be complacent, or imagine that creationism is just a bizarre and distant American phenomenon. Just as manipulative as the worst of American creationists, European creationists are hard at work and some of them have a lot of money (Oktar also sent his book to many universities in the US). What we have seen so far is just the beginning.

As the bicentenary of Darwin's birth and 150th anniversary of the publication of *On the Origin of Species* coincide in 2009, those of us who support science have an excellent opportunity to reclaim the agenda. To be successful we need interdisciplinary collaboration across all branches of science and the humanities. The issue at stake is not just a question of ideologically motivated attacks on the theory of evolution. At the very heart of the debate lies the question of the standing of academic knowledge in society. We need to take this seriously, both in the humanities and in the sciences. Now more than ever it is time to bridge the gap and together stop the nonsense.

In Europe, Creationism Is Defended

Daniel Steinvorth and Harun Yahya

In the following interview with Spiegel *magazine reporter Daniel Steinvorth, Turkish creationist Harun Yahya (also known as Adnan Oktar) argues that the theory of evolution is untrue. He charges that Darwinism is being protected worldwide by governments. He further opines that Muslims who commit terrorist acts are actually Darwinists only pretending to be Muslims. He also predicts that people will soon understand that Darwinism is a plot by Satan. Yahya is the author of* Atlas of Creation.

As you read, consider the following questions:

1. For how long does Harun Yahya say Darwinists deceived the whole of humanity?
2. Yahya asserts that Darwinism has laid the foundation for what three dictators?
3. Of what crime has Yahya been accused in Turkish courts?

[**D**aniel Steinvorth]: *Virtually every respected biologist in the world considers the theory of evolution as perhaps the best-proven scientific theory ever, on par with the knowledge that the world is round. How do you want to prove them wrong?*

Adnan Oktar [Harun Yahya]: First of all, there are 100 million fossils that prove creation. And these have never

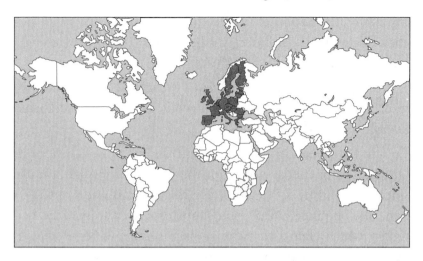

changed in any respect. For example, fish have always been fish, shrimp have always been shrimp, and crabs have always been crabs. And their fossils are on display in every corner of the world. We displayed them in Turkey as well, and people saw them with their own eyes. First and foremost, this is a clear proof. Secondly, in contrast to creation, Darwinism does not have a single piece of evidence demonstrating the theory of evolution. Its proponents don't have any fossil evidence, of the kind which they should be able to put forward.

Last year, the Council of Europe even asked its member states not to teach creationism along with the theory of evolution in schools. Do you consider this a defeat?

"Darwinism does not have a single piece of evidence demonstrating the theory of evolution."

Darwinism is under official protection throughout the world. No other ideology in history, no other idea, has ever been kept under such strict official protection. To make any kind of statement criticizing Darwinism causes an official re-action. However, the invalidity of Darwinism and the actuality of creation are scientific facts. Anyone reading or looking over my *Atlas of Creation* arrives at this opinion. Darwinism lies about many issues and deceives humanity. They have deceived the whole of humanity for 150 years.

How much were you influenced by Christian movements, the so-called intelligent design movements in Europe and the United States?

I find the concept of intelligent design rather dishonest. One should openly stand up for the existence of Allah, should sincerely stand up for religion, for Islam. Or, if one is a Christian, one should honestly stand up for Christianity. This is a theory which claims that things have somehow been created, but it is unknown who created them. I find this rather dishonest, actually. The followers of intelligent design should openly and clearly declare the existence of Allah as the Creator.

Richard Dawkins, one of the most prominent figures of the new atheism, recently had his book The God Delusion *translated into Turkish. In Turkey, 15,000 copies were reportedly sold. In it, he writes that religion is one of the causes of terrorism.*

"The followers of intelligent design should openly and clearly declare the existence of Allah as the Creator."

Darwinism has laid the groundwork for [Adolf] Hitler's and [Benito] Mussolini's fascism and [Joseph] Stalin's communism. And when we look at the present day, we see that all the members of terrorist organizations—even those that portray themselves as Muslim organizations—are Darwinists, atheists. That is to say, a faithful person who prays regularly does not go and plant bombs here and there. It is just people who pretend to be Muslims, those who depict themselves as Muslims, who perpetrate bombings, or Darwinists who make it clear that they are terrorists or communists who commit terrorism. Consequently, they are all Darwinists.

Creationism Makes European Inroads

Creationism is still a marginal issue here compared with its impact on cultural and political debate in the United States. But the budding fervor is part of a growing embrace of evangelical worship throughout much of Europe. Evangelicals say their ranks are swelling as attendance at traditional churches declines because of revulsion with the hedonism and materialism of modern society.

"People are looking for spirituality," [Monty] White said in an interview at his [Answers in Genesis] office in Leicester, 90 miles north of London. "I think they are fed up with not finding true happiness. They find having a bigger car doesn't make them happy. They get drunk and the next morning they have a hangover. They take drugs but the drugs wear off. But what they find with Christianity is lasting."

Other British organizations have joined the crusade. A group called Truth in Science has sent thousands of unsolicited DVDs to every high school in Britain arguing that mankind is the result of "intelligent design," not Darwinian evolution.

Gregory Katz,
"Creationism vs. Evolution Battle Flares in Europe,"
USA Today, *February 11, 2008. www.usatoday.com.*

Do you really think that someone like Osama bin Laden, who justifies terrorist acts using the Koran and the alleged ungodliness of the West, is following Darwinist ideas?

Things are not what they seem to be. You do not see that appearance and style in such people in their youth. Yet, when their actual faith is scrutinized, it emerges that they are genuine materialists and Darwinists. It is impossible for a person who fears Allah to commit terrorist acts because of his faith. Such acts are committed by people who were educated abroad, who received a Darwinist education and who internalized Darwinism, but who later called themselves Muslims. When scrutinized carefully, when their speech and essays are carefully analyzed, we see that all these people are Darwinists.

Speaking of Hitler and fascism: On your Web site, you condemn the Holocaust and link it to Darwinism. But, in the early 1990s, you published a book about the so-called "Holocaust Lie."

"[Terrorist] acts are committed by people who were educated abroad, who received a Darwinist education and who internalized Darwinism, but later called themselves Muslims."

The book, *The Holocaust Lie*, is by one of my friends, Nuri Özbudak. It is not one of my books. He published his own essays under that title. Later, we protested against this through the Public Notary and declared the fact to the public. I did not take any other legal action but only protested through the Public Notary because he used my name. My book expressing my own ideas was published later.

Next year [2009], a part of the world will celebrate the 200th anniversary of Darwin's birth and the 150th anniversary of his first publication of On the Origin of Species. *Will you be celebrating, too?*

It will actually turn out to be a worldwide celebration of Darwinism's collapse. People will be stunned at how they believed in Darwinism. They will be amazed at how they were taken in by such a hoax for years. They will also be astonished at themselves and at how hundreds, thousands of universities around the world and hundreds, thousands of professors backed such a hoax, and how they were deceived by Satan's plot.

One of your books is called Atlas of Creation, *a massive and obviously very expensive volume. It was distributed all over the world, and many free copies were sent to members of the Western media. How do you finance your struggle against Darwinism?*

The publishing house makes a great profit, since I do not take any royalties from my books. And my books are being sold in great numbers both domestically and abroad. Last year, 8 million copies were sold in Turkey and 2 million abroad. This makes a considerable total sum. Almost no other book has ever sold so much in Turkey. This year it is even higher; it is many times higher. Sales have doubled. It is perfectly normal for the publishing house to use part of that income to distribute books. This counts as publicity. However, the financial resources for this, as I have stated, are supplied by the publishing house.

In May, you were sentenced by a Turkish court for having created an illegal organization for personal gain.

Yes, there had been an allegation of a criminal organization. Yes, I was accused of being a gang leader. I have been given a penalty of three years' imprisonment. This needs to be ratified by the Supreme Court of Appeals. If the Supreme Court of Appeals ratifies this verdict, I will be given three years' imprisonment. However, there is no legal evidence in the sense that I understand to be acceptable. Since my deposition was taken without my lawyer present, it should be invalid. My deposition—which I was made to give under coercion, by force—has been accepted (as) valid both in the Supreme Court of Appeals and also in the court. Thus, I have been given this sentence.

In Canada, Religious Beliefs Can Be Overridden by End-of-Life Medical Decisions

Jonathan Rosenblum

In the following viewpoint, Jonathan Rosenblum reports on the case of Samuel Golubchuk (also known as Chaim Schmuel Golubchuk), a Canadian Jewish man whose doctors wanted to remove him from life support. Rosenblum notes that in Canada, doctors have the sole authority to make decisions about end-of-life treatment, which empowers them to make decisions contrary to a patient's religious beliefs or the wishes of the patient's family. Rosenblum cautions that people should be afraid of "the claim of moral omniscience" made by doctors in the Canadian medical system. Rosenblum discusses some of the history of Social Darwinism and the eugenics program under Hitler to show how doctors then were influenced by ideology. Rosenblum suggests that modern "quality of life" arguments reflect beliefs and promote actions similar to those of Social Darwinism. Rosenblum is the director of Jewish Media Resources.

As you read, consider the following questions:

1. What were the doctors of Samuel Golubchuk prepared to do to expedite the death of their patient, according to Jonathan Rosenblum?
2. Who is Dr. Jeff Blackner, according to the viewpoint?

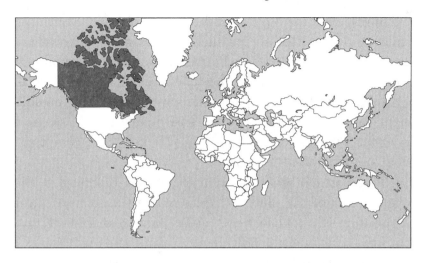

3. What are the similarities between the modern view of "quality of life" and the beliefs of Social Darwinism that reached their culmination under Hitler, according to the viewpoint?

A Winnipeg case currently winding its way to its grim conclusion pits the children of Samuel Golubchuk against doctors at the Salvation Army Grace General Hospital. According to the pleadings, Golubchuk's doctors informed his children that their 84-year-old father is "in the process of dying" and that they intended to hasten the process by removing his ventilation, and if that proved insufficient to kill him quickly, to also remove his feeding tube. In the event that the patient showed discomfort during these procedures, the chief of the hospital's ICU unit stated in his affidavit that he would administer morphine.

Golubchuk is an Orthodox Jew, as are his children. The latter have adamantly opposed his removal from the ventilator and feeding tube, on the grounds that Jewish law expressly forbids any action designed to shorten life, and that if their father could express his wishes, he would oppose the doctors acting to deliberately terminate his life.

In response, the director of the ICU informed Golubchuk's children that neither their father's wishes nor their own are relevant, and he would do whatever he decided was appropriate. Bill Olson, counsel for the ICU director, told the Canadian Broadcasting Company that physicians have the sole right to make decisions about treatment—even if it goes against a patient's religious beliefs—and that "there is no right to a continuation of treatment."

That position was supported by Dr. Jeff Blackner, executive director of the office of ethics of the Canadian Medical Association. He told Reuters: "[W]e want to make sure that clinical decisions are left to physicians and not judges." Doctors' decisions are made only with the "best interest of the individual patient at heart," he said, though he did not explain how that could be squared with the undisputed claim that this patient would oppose the doctors' decision. Meanwhile, an Angus Reid poll of Canadians showed that 68% supported leaving the final decision with the family.

"Bill Olson, counsel for the ICU director, told the Canadian Broadcasting Company that physicians have the sole right to make decisions about treatment—even if it goes against a patient's religious beliefs—and that 'there is no right to a continuation of treatment.'"

The claim of absolute physician discretion to withdraw life-support advanced by the Canadian doctors would spell the end of any patient autonomy over end-of-life decisions. So-called living wills, which are recognized in many American states, and which allow a person to specify in advance who should make such decisions in the event of their incapacity, would be rendered nugatory.

Even those who would not wish to be maintained in a state of unconsciousness, and who do not share the religious beliefs of the Golubchuk family should fear the claim of moral

The Right to Live

I'd like to venture into another end-of-life-care matter related to the late [Chaim Shmuel] Sam Golubchuk, of blessed memory. He is the Winnipeg man who wanted to live, who wanted to be treated so he could continue to live. He had suffered brain damage and was in a compromised state, but he was still able to communicate with his family in some manner. . . .

There is a myth about this case that needs to be addressed. The fight that Sam's children waged on his behalf was not about imposing Jewish law on Canadian society. It was about the right to live, which is a most fundamental human right. The fact that most Canadians in Sam's state might have opted for being kept comfortable is totally irrelevant. What is relevant is that Sam—for reasons that he, like everyone else, is entitled to—wanted to live. No one had a right to deny him, or anyone else, that choice, that right.

Reuven Bulka,
"Destroying Jewish Myths About Organ Donation,"
Canadian Jewish News, *July 16, 2008. www.cjnews.com.*

omniscience made by Canadian doctors—and not just because Josef Mengele was a doctor. As Professor Richard Weikart chillingly details in *From Darwin to Hitler: Evolutionary Ethics, Eugenics, and Racism in Germany,* Mengele's experiments on "inferior" Jewish children for the benefit of the Master Race have to be viewed in the context of German Social Darwinism in the seven decades leading up to the Nazi takeover.

In Weikart's estimate, a majority of German physicians and scientists subscribed to the naturalistic Darwinian world view and ideas that constituted a sustained assault on the traditional Judeo-Christian concept of the sanctity of life. Among those ideas are the claim that there is no fundamental distinction between humans and animals; human beings do not possess a soul that endows them with any rights or superiority to any other species; within the species homo sapiens, there are "inferior" and "superior" individuals, and inferior and superior races; and it is the iron will of nature that the species should evolve through the survival of the superior members and the death of the inferior.

Darwin's cousin Francis Galton founded the modern eugenics movement on the basis of Darwinian arguments, and nowhere did eugenics catch on with greater enthusiasm than in Germany (though many prominent intellectuals in the United States, England and France were also enthusiastic supporters). In Germany, many took the next step—from eugenics to involuntary euthanasia for the mentally ill and other defectives.

"In place of the sanctity of life, we now speak of the 'quality of life'—a term that explicitly assumes that some lives are worth more than others."

Ernest Haeckel, one of the most influential 19th-century German biologists, whose faked drawings of developing human embryos allegedly recapitulating the evolutionary path still feature prominently in college biology texts, argued for the killing of the mentally ill, lepers, those with incurable cancer, and cretins. As a safeguard, he too recommended a committee of physicians to pass judgment. Alfred Hoche, a professor of psychiatry at the University of Freiburg, justified shortening an inferior life if the insights gained would save better lives. "By giving up the conception of the divine image of humans under the influence of Darwinian thinkers," writes

Hans-Walter Schmuhl, mainstream German thinkers came to view human life as "a piece of property" to be weighed against other pieces of property.

Just as Nazism gave anti-Semitism a bad name, so too did it discredit Social Darwinism. But just as anti-Semitism has reappeared, so has the assault on the concept of the sanctity of life. That assault is not limited to Princeton ethicist Peter Singer's defense of infanticide, euthanasia and bestiality on explicitly Darwinian grounds.

Global warming activists speak of the duty not to reproduce, and view human beings as the enemy of nature's order. So much for the view of man as the crown of creation. In place of the sanctity of life, we now speak of the "quality of life"—a term that explicitly assumes that some lives are worth more than others.

There is even talk of the "duty to die" and clear the way for higher-quality lives, which is why the American Association of People with Disabilities has been actively involved in so many cases dealing with the doctors' right to terminate medical care. The rage for medical rationing in Canada, of which the Golubchuk case is but one example, derives from a desire not to waste resources on low-quality lives.

It would be a bitter irony if Percy Shulman, a Jewish judge in Winnipeg, were to grant Dr. Bojan Paunovic the right to end Samuel Golubchuk's life on the grounds that it lacks the requisite quality.

Periodical Bibliography

*The following articles have been selected to supplement the
diverse views presented in this chapter.*

Craig Brown	"Science Works Like Clockwork, Religion Floats with Clouds," *Scotsman*, February 20, 2008.
Larry Churchill	"The Dangers of Looking for the Health Benefits of Religion," *Lancet*, May 5, 2007.
Astrid Dinter and Peter Schreiner	"Science and Religion in Schools: A German and World Wide Perspective," *Global Spiral*, June 3, 2008. www.metanexus.net.
Global Agenda	"Questions of Faith: The Christian Church: Catholics, Anglicans and Other Christians All Still Different About Where the Divide Between Faith and Reason Lies," April 10, 2007.
Global Agenda	"Where Angels No Longer Fear to Tread: How Scientists Try to Explain the Existence of Religion," March 23, 2008.
Jeffrey Kluger	"How Faith Can Heal," *TIME*, February 23, 2009.
Guy Lengagne	"The Dangers of Creationism in Education," Council of Europe Parliamentary Assembly, June 8, 2007. http://assembly.coe.int.
Harry Morris III	"Where Evolution Has Gaps, Creation Might Offer Answers—If We Will Listen," *U.S. News & World Report*, February 2, 2009. www.usnews.com.
Elliott Sober	"What Is Wrong with Intelligent Design?" *Quarterly Review of Biology*, vol. 82, no. 1, March 2007.
David Sloan Wilson	"Beyond Demonic Memes: Why Richard Dawkins Is Wrong About Religion," *eSkeptic*, July 4, 2007. www.skeptic.com.

GLOBALVIEWPOINTS

CHAPTER 3

Religion and Politics

Religious Fundamentalism May Decline in Iran

Sadegh Zibakalam

In the following viewpoint, Sadegh Zibakalam predicts that militant Islam will decline in Iran over the next decade. He argues that although hardline militants have been in power since 2005, their performance in office has turned the educated and middle classes against them. Under the militants, according to Zibakalam, Iran has suffered from inflation, unemployment, and the loss of the professional class to emigration. As a consequence, it is likely that a more moderate government will be elected, according to the author. Zibakalam is a professor of political science at Tehran University in Iran.

As you read, consider the following questions:

1. In what countries does the author of this viewpoint suggest the consequences of radical Islam can be observed?

2. With whom has Tehran tried to establish ties, according to this viewpoint?

3. Whom did the Iranian parliament elect as speaker in July 2008?

During the past three decades the rise of militant Islam has in many ways dominated political events in the region. The consequences of Iranian religious radicalism can be

Sadegh Zibakalam, "The Decline of Religious Fundamentalism in Iran," *Bitter Lemons International*, vol. 6, no. 41, November 6, 2008. Copyright © 2008 Bitterlemons International. Reproduced by permission.

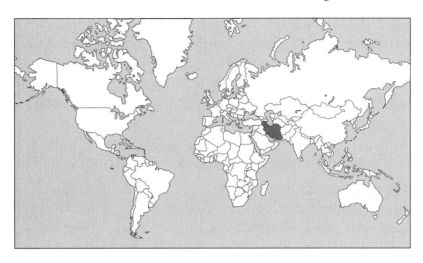

observed in the Persian Gulf region, in the Arab-Israel conflict, in Iraq and in Afghanistan. Although Iranian Islamic militancy appears to be as dominant as ever, this may not be the case during the next decade.

"Although Iranian Islamic militancy appears to be as dominant as ever, this may not be the case during the next decade."

The main reason for this conjuncture lies with the present Iranian government headed by President Mahmoud Ahmadinejad, who came to power in July 2005. Ahmadinejad's rise to power was indeed a watershed in post-Islamic revolution Iran. His presidency marked a new political configuration in the Islamic republic. Hitherto, although the Iranian regime was described as radical and Islamic, it was far from a united political group. It consisted of diverse currents that all described themselves as Islamist. They included hardline conservatives on the "right", the "left", the pragmatists headed by Akbar Hashemi Rafsanjani, the moderates and those who with some qualification could even be described as "liberal". During the reign of the late Imam Khomeini the left had the upper hand. After his death, the pragmatists headed by Hashemi Rafsanjani held the center stage; then it was the turn of the moderate-liberal currents headed by the reformist president, Mohammad Khatami. No matter who had been elected as Iran's president, all the other currents were, albeit to various degrees, present in the government.

A Changing Political Complexion in Iran

The elections of July 2005 and the rise of Ahmadinejad to power changed that political complexion. The conservative hardliners purged almost all the other currents from power. For the first time since the emergence of the Islamic republic in 1979, one particular political group dominated the main three branches of the Iranian political establishment.

This group, which with some justification has become known as the hardliners, has tried to change much of Iranian domestic as well as foreign policy. At the international level, Iran's stand on its nuclear program has become much more uncompromising. The Islamic regime's anti-Western and anti-American attitude has intensified, as has its anti-Israel approach. Instead, Tehran has tried to establish ties with anti-American regimes in South America and elsewhere. Internally, the hardliners have intensified the state's role in the economy and curtailed political freedom and have tried to expand the country's military capabilities.

We come now to the main point of our thesis: the anticipated demise of militant Islam during the next decade. Given the widespread grip on power that the hardliners have maintained since 2005, why should their power decline in the future? The short answer lies with the performance of the hardliners since they came to power three years ago. They have alienated much of the country's intelligentsia. Students, university graduates, professionals, intellectuals, writers, journalists, artists and many similar social groups have turned increasingly critical of the hardliners' overall policies during the

---

Key Facts About Iran

- Population: 66,429,284

- 68% of the population lives in urban areas

- 98% of the population is Muslim

- Of these, 89% are Shia and 9% are Sunni

- 58% of the population speaks Persian

- 26% of the population speaks Turkic and Turkic dialects

- 9% of the population speaks Kurdish

- Capital city: Tehran

- Government: theocratic republic

CIA, The World Factbook, June 1, 2009.
www.cia.gov/library/publications/the-world-factbook/geos/IR.html.

---

past three years [since 2005]. Civil servants, the urban middle class and the politically powerful bazaar merchants have increasingly turned against the hardliner government of Ahmadinejad.

"Students, university graduates, professionals, intellectuals, writers, journalists, artists and many similar social groups have turned increasingly critical of the hardliners' overall policies [since 2005]."

Hardliners in Retreat

Politically, too, the hardliners have been in retreat. The reformists, the left, the so-called liberal-religious nationalist groups such as "Nehzat Azadi", Hashemi Rafsanjani and his influential political groups, all now oppose the hardliner government. In fact, Ahmadinejad's policies have turned many conservatives as well as more moderate and pragmatist hardliners against his government. There is yet another powerful and influential group that has become openly critical of the hardliner president and some of his decisions: During the past two years, a number of senior clerical leaders have voiced their opposition to some of Ahmadinejad's decisions.

Last but by no means least is the Iranian parliament, or Majlis. The 300-member assembly that was inaugurated in July 2008 elected Ali Larijani by a large majority as its speaker. Since the conservatives have a considerable majority in the present Majlis, Larijani's election was an implicit message of defiance to President Ahmadinejad. Larijani was until last April head of the High Council of Security Affairs, a powerful body that is responsible for the country's military and security issues, including conducting negotiations with the International Atomic Energy Agency. Larijani was critical of Ahmadinejad's radical approach regarding Iran's nuclear program. He preferred a more moderate stand, searching for compromise with the West on the nuclear issue. Ahmadinejad dismissed Larijani, thereby eventually paving the way for Iran to adopt a more militant and confrontational approach vis-à-vis its nuclear program.

Here we must address two important questions about the hardline government of Iran. First, given his formidable internal opposition, where does Ahmadinejad get the support to survive and even to contemplate another term? Second, what are the reasons for so much opposition?

Ahmadinejad's Poor Performance

The bulk of Ahmadinejad's support comes from the supreme leader, Ayatollah Ali Khamenei and the various institutions he leads, including the powerful Revolutionary Guards, the Baseej, the National Iranian Radio & Television and government-run newspapers, as well as a number of religious and political leaders close to him. The widespread opposition stems from Ahmadinejad's overall poor performance. The country suffers from rampant inflation; unemployment hasn't come down, nor has endemic corruption and the country's brain drain continues—witness the queue of Iranian professionals outside western embassies in Tehran, seeking to emigrate in spite of the fact that the country's oil revenues have quadrupled during the past three years.

It was against this irony that Hashemi Rafsanjani, the leading moderate Iranian leader, warned last month that the failure of the present government would not simply constitute the defeat of a particular political group but rather would be interpreted as the failure in practice of radical Islam when it had all the power at its disposal.

The Russian Government Restricts Religious Freedom

Geraldine Fagan

In the following viewpoint, Geraldine Fagan summarizes the state of religious freedom in Russia. She argues that the Russian government's attempt to combat religious extremism is leading to restrictions and harassment of religious groups. These restrictions include, according to Fagan, the prohibition of religious tracts deemed extremist; the dissolution of religious groups for holding educational activities; and the denial of visas for religious workers. The government is also taking over property from religious groups, leaving them without a location to worship. Fagan is a writer for Forum 18.

As you read, consider the following questions:

1. What would be the effect of the Asbest Town Court's banning of Jehovah's Witness literature, according to Fagan?
2. Why was a Pentecostal Bible Centre in Chuvashia dissolved in 2007, according to Geraldine Fagan?
3. What two religious groups are waging a bureaucratic battle for approval to build places of worship?

Geraldine Fagan, "Russia: Religious Freedom Survey," *Forum 18 News*, October 2008. Reproduced by permission of Forum 18 News Service www.forum18.org.

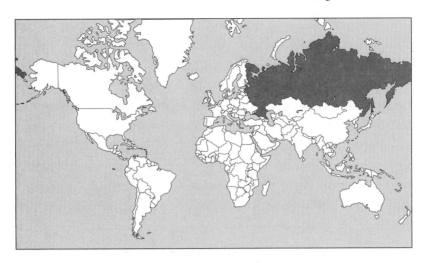

Without doubt the gravest current threat to freedom of religion or belief in Russia comes from the federal government's approach to combating religious extremism. The June 2002 Extremism Law's lengthy definition of extremism contains a number of clauses describing such activity in a religious context: incitement of religious hatred; propaganda of the exclusivity, superiority or inferiority of citizens according to their attitude towards religion or religious affiliation; obstruction of the lawful activity of religious associations accompanied by violence or the threat of violence; committing a crime motivated by religious hatred.

The Implementation of the Extremism Law

While such formulations are quite defensible, the government's record in seeking to apply them has caused grave concern to some. For local human rights defenders, the February 2003 ban of the radical Islamic group Hizb-ut-Tahrir prompted alarm about how the law was being implemented. Hizb-ut-Tahrir's Web site has voiced virulently anti-Semitic views warranting prosecution under the 2002 Extremism Law. . . . Russia, however, chose to outlaw the group as a terrorist organisation, in a closed session of the Supreme Court whose verdict did not cite evidence of terrorist activity.

Subsequent prosecutions of dozens of alleged Hizb-ut-Tahrir members across Russia hinged not on proven participation in terrorist acts, or even membership of the organisation, but the content of the group's literature alleged to have been circulated by suspects. In a 2005 case in Tobolsk (Tyumen Region), for instance, five young Muslims were handed down sentences ranging up to six years for extremism, as well as aiding and abetting terrorism, solely on the basis of literary evidence.

"The right ... to criticise religious and non-religious beliefs of all kinds is, in international human rights law, a fundamental part of the right to religious freedom."

The Hizb-ut-Tahrir texts in question were not those whose content invites prosecution for religious extremism, however, and the experts whose analysis secured convictions did not identify such elements. Rather, in assessing this literature, a former scientific atheism lecturer concluded that its "call to the universal Islamisation of humanity signifies nothing less than propaganda for coups d'état and violent change in the state and order of every country." Vladimir Viktorov [a professor at Maksim Gorky Urals State University] also maintained that the literature "propagandises the idea of the superiority of Islam, and therefore Muslims, over other religions and the people who adhere to them."

This latter assertion features prominently in every subsequent ban or attempt to ban allegedly religious extremist literature. . . . Its flaw is to confuse claims that those citizens holding a particular belief are superior—which is defined as extremism by the 2002 law—with claims that a particular religious or non-religious belief itself is superior to other beliefs. The right to be able to make this kind of claim and to criticise religious and non-religious beliefs of all kinds is, in international human rights law, a fundamental part of the right to religious freedom. . . .

The Case Against Jehovah's Witnesses

In late 2007, the authorities in Rostov-on-Don Region ordered investigations into local communities of Jehovah's Witnesses after an expert literary analysis declared some of their well-known tracts extremist. In May 2008, the public prosecutor's office in the town of Asbest (Sverdlovsk Region) issued warnings to a local Jehovah's Witness community on the same grounds.

While a district court in the Russian capital failed to find the Jehovah's Witnesses' local religious organisation in Moscow guilty of extremism, it succeeded in banning it on other grounds in 2004. The Jehovah's Witnesses made an appeal against this long-running prosecution to the European Court of Human Rights (ECHR) on 11 December 2001, updated by supplementary material on 15 December 2004. The ECHR has yet to pronounce on the admissibility of the complaint.

Despite the ban, Moscow Jehovah's Witnesses have broadly been able to function under the legal umbrella of their federal organisation. While they have faced some rental restrictions and occasional impediment to their preaching activity, their summer 2007 stadium congress in the Russian capital met with no obstruction, for example. However, if Asbest Town Court—or any other court—were to succeed in banning Jehovah's Witness literature as extremist, this would prevent its distribution across Russia and could even lead to a ban on the federal organisation and all its affiliates.

The authorities have recently stepped up their action against Jehovah's Witnesses in other ways, too. In what the organisation's representatives describe as an unprecedented, coordinated campaign in 2008, state officials prevented at least eight Jehovah's Witness regional summer congresses from taking place, while a further 30 went ahead despite similar attempts to obstruct them. Previously, a handful of congresses were blocked or disrupted in 2003-5, but all went ahead in 2007.

In cases where the ECHR has found against Russia on a religious freedom issue, the state has subsequently paid compensation in full. The Moscow branch of the Salvation Army, a community of Jehovah's Witnesses in the Urals city of Chelyabinsk and an evangelical church in Chekhov (Moscow Region) all received such payments in 2007. However, in the case of the Salvation Army—the only one where the legal situation which led to the violation could be changed—Russia has taken no action, even though this is an ECHR requirement. The Salvation Army thus continues to function in Moscow using the legal personality status it had before the 1997 Religion Law, as this has not been annulled as was threatened. However, it is still unable to re-register in line with that law, as the deadline has expired. . . .

Religious Education Is Restricted

In some cases, a functioning religious organisation may find itself dissolved for educational activity which local officials believe should be licensed. A Pentecostal Bible Centre in Chuvashia was dissolved for unlicensed educational activity in August 2007 and has subsequently sent an appeal to the ECHR. In January 2008, FSB [Federal Security Service] officers broke up an Embassy of God Bible School graduation ceremony in Tolyatti (Samara Region), claiming that the church requires a licence for educational activity. In March 2008, Smolensk Regional Court dissolved Smolensk United Methodist Church for running a Sunday school—which has only four pupils— for not having an education licence.

Confusion has persisted over what type of religious activity requires such a licence. The 1997 law distinguishes between "education"—for which a religious organisation appears to re-

Russian Antagonism Toward Religious Organizations

[Russian] Legislators have identified religious organizations as particularly prone to exhibit extremist characteristics. The antagonism of Russian legislators toward foreign religious organizations follows in part from Russia's slow acceptance of concepts underlying Western religious pluralism. The appearance of financially-robust foreign religious groups during the liberalized period of the early 1990s contributed to embittered perceptions by the financially-ailing Russian Orthodox Church and its followers that foreign groups were "purchasing souls" at the expense of Russian culture. Consequently, many perceive religious pluralism as a betrayal of "Russianness" and the Orthodox Church's "spiritual rights to Russia."

On a more general level, there are widespread perceptions that foreign religious organizations and new religious movements defraud the spiritually feeble, brainwash vulnerable youth, weaken family affections, discourage fulfillment of citizens' responsibilities, and, in some cases, even use religion as a cover for espionage. Most of these perceptions are remnants of deeply engrained stereotypes that stigmatize unfamiliar religious traditions as "cults" and "sects." The understandable response of closely monitoring socially dangerous groups has unfortunately led to broad restrictions that tend to adversely affect many legitimate religious organizations that are not traditionally Russian.

Brian J. Gross,
"Russia's War on Political and Religious Extremism:
An Appraisal of the Law on Counteracting Extremist Activity,"
Brigham Young University Law Review, *2003.*

quire a licence—and "teaching", for which it definitely does not. Quashing Smolensk Regional Court's verdict against the local Smolensk church in a landmark 10 June 2008 ruling, Russia's Supreme Court determined that a licence is required for educational activity if "accompanied by confirmation that the student has attained levels of education prescribed by the state." A yeshiva (Jewish school) which the Moscow city authorities announced in March 2008 would be dissolved, for not having an educational licence, now hopes that it will legally be able to continue its activity as "teaching".

In recent years there have been complaints by non-Orthodox parents—with different or no religious beliefs—that the Foundations of Orthodox Culture course in state schools is compulsory catechetical education, rather than voluntary cultural education. Provision of the course across Russia is patchy. Its imposition has gone furthest in Belgorod Region, where it was introduced as a compulsory subject for all pupils in 2006. In September 2007, however, then President Vladimir Putin publicly rejected this approach while on a visit to Belgorod. He stated that: "Our Constitution says that the Church is separate from the state. You know how I feel, including towards the Russian Orthodox Church. But if anyone thinks that we should proceed differently, that would require a change to the Constitution. I do not believe that is what we should be doing now." While it is unclear how the situation will develop, the federal authorities are now unlikely to support anything more than strictly optional study of religious subjects.

Religious Workers Are Denied Visas

The Ukrainian pastor of a Kiev-based charismatic church was deported from a Moscow airport in February 2008, but no further cases of visa denials or deportations of foreign religious personnel are known ... from the past two years. Over 50 foreign religious workers—including Catholics, Protestants, Muslims, Buddhists and a Jew—have been barred from Russia since 1998. A small number of those who had earlier been barred have since managed to return.

While not targeted at religious communities, new visa rules introduced in October 2007 allowing foreigners with a business or humanitarian visa—which includes religious work—to spend only 90 out of every 180 days in Russia have had a harsh impact on many religious organisations, particularly those which for historical reasons depend upon foreigners, such as the Catholic Church. The difficulties are avoidable, but the procedures for obtaining temporary residency or a work permit—which allow an unbroken stay in Russia—are lengthy and time consuming.

"Over 50 foreign religious workers—including Catholics, Protestants, Muslims, Buddhists and a Jew—have been barred from Russia since 1998."

Religious Groups Have Property Problems

A major problem for all confessions, in varying degrees, continues to be the acquisition or retention of places of worship. A new factor in such situations is commercial pressures, particularly in the economically more successful parts of Russia. In the Far Eastern city of Khabarovsk, for example, a parish of the Russian Orthodox Church was forced out of a historical church in October 2007 when the hospital complex to which it belongs was bought by a commercial enterprise. In Kaluga, Word of Life Pentecostal Church has similarly come under sustained pressure after it found its land and building surrounded by the construction of a shopping centre.

In other cases, places of worship are threatened when officials question whether they have been built with proper approval or to safety standards, in what the religious communities concerned believe to be a pretext for harassment. In the southern city of Astrakhan, demolition of an unfinished mosque was postponed in 2007 due to a case pending at the European Court of Human Rights. In the Siberian republic of Khakassia, however, Glorification Pentecostal Church was forced to demolish its prayer hall in June 2007.

In Moscow, Molokans (an indigenous Russian Christian confession), the Hare Krishna community and Emmanuel Pentecostal Church are waging long-running bureaucratic battles for approval to construct houses of worship. Other groups, such as an Old Believer parish in Tambov Region, continue to face obstruction in trying to reclaim their historical places of worship.

Religious Freedom of Expression Is Threatened Worldwide

AC Grayling

In the following viewpoint, AC Grayling warns that attempts by the Organisation of the Islamic Conference (OIC) to ban the defamation of religion could lead to serious infringements of freedom of speech. He asserts that if the group is successful, journalists will not be able to criticize the pope for his views on contraception or condemn Islamic governments for their brutal punishment of women. He concludes that the reason the OIC wants to change the Universal Declaration of Human Rights is because religion often violates those rights. Grayling is a professor of philosophy at the University of London.

As you read, consider the following questions:

1. What punishment did Saudi Arabia exact from a 74-year-old woman who had two male visitors who were not her relatives?
2. To what can the pope's attitude toward sex be attributed, according to AC Grayling?
3. What principle does Grayling argue should be entrenched and made effective?

Facts speak for themselves. Omid Reza Mir Sayafi, 29, a journalist and blogger, has taken his own life in Evin prison in Iran, where he was serving a two-year sentence for "insulting Ayatollahs Khomeini and Khamenei", and awaiting further trial for "insulting sacred values", which would have meant more years in prison. He was a sensitive man, who blogged mainly about music and the arts, and imprisonment was a hellish experience for him; he was reported to be profoundly depressed and anxious.

Sayafi is yet another victim of religion. If the Organisation of the Islamic Conference (OIC) has its way, it will become impossible to make such a remark.

"At the United Nations Council on Human Rights. . .the OIC [Organisation of the Islamic Conference] is trying again to have 'defamation of religion' banned. The aim is a universal gag on free speech."

A Potential Gag on Free Speech

At the United Nations Council on Human Rights in Geneva, the OIC is trying again to have "defamation of religion" banned. The aim is a universal gag on free speech, blocking the right of anyone to criticise the too frequently negative effects of religion on individuals and society. The OIC has yet to appreciate that if it succeeds in its effort to protect Islam from legitimate challenges to its less attractive doctrines and practices—to say nothing of Islamism with its murderous extreme—the relentless anti-Semitism from its own side of the street will have to stop, too.

If it succeeds in turning criticism of religion and its main beneficiaries into "defamation", we might not be free to express our condemnation of a sentence just handed down in Saudi Arabia against a 74-year-old woman, condemned to 45 lashes, three months in prison, and deportation to her native Jordan, for having two male visitors in her home who were not relatives.

The Pope's Views Are Condemned

And here is another thing we might not be able to discuss. The pope's iteration of his church's doctrine on contraception, while on his way to visit Africa where 21 million people in sub-Saharan countries are infected with HIV, millions have died of AIDS, and millions of AIDS orphans live in frightful conditions of semi-slavery and destitution, has been rightly condemned by many around the world.

But the HIV/AIDS tragedy of Africa is only the tip of an iceberg. Opposition to control of family size in the poorest part of the world condemns women to endless pregnancies if they are not—as many are—killed or incapacitated by child-bearing in difficult circumstances. The difficulty of looking after numerous children in abject poverty is, on its own, a grinding oppression, to say nothing of the immense barriers to the opportunity for decent lives later on for the children. These brutal facts are as nothing to the pope: In his view the blight of too many pregnancies, too many children, infant mortality, starvation, disease, poverty and immiseration is all part of the deity's plan. For anyone who goes by evidence, if there is a deity, this suggests that it devotes its spare time to pulling wings off flies.

The pope's attitude to sex is mainly informed by having to deal with child-abusing priests (latest reports say that in the US complaints against abusive priests rose to 800 in 2008: that's more than a dozen a week), which is why his advice to them—abstinence—seems to be the only thing he can think to suggest to everyone else, and most of all as a guard against HIV infection. Plenty of people lack insight into the deep imperatives of human nature, so let us not blame the pope for adding this particular deficit to his already rich repertoire of

The Universal Declaration of Human Rights of the United Nations, Adopted December 10, 1948

Now, Therefore THE GENERAL ASSEMBLY proclaims THIS UNIVERSAL DECLARATION OF HUMAN RIGHTS as a common standard of achievement for all peoples and all nations, to the end that every individual and every organ of society, keeping this Declaration constantly in mind, shall strive by teaching and education to promote respect for these rights and freedoms and by progressive measures, national and international, to secure their universal and effective recognition and observance, both among the peoples of Member States themselves and among the peoples of territories under their jurisdiction. . . .

Article 18.

• Everyone has the right to freedom of thought, conscience and religion; this right includes freedom to change his religion or belief, and freedom, either alone or in community with others and in public or private, to manifest his religion or belief in teaching, practice, worship and observance.

The Universal Declaration of Human Rights,
The United Nations, December 10, 1948.
www.un.org.

them: But let us ask whether a marrying clergy might not be part of the solution to sexually abusing priests, if there has to be a clergy at all. Best of all as a policy for the pope and his church on matters of sex might be silence. To adapt [philosopher Ludwig] Wittgenstein, "Wherof you know nothing, shut up."

The chief point is that Vatican policy on contraception is in every sense a hideous crime against humanity and ought to be treated as such.

Religion Violates Human Rights

And that takes us back to the OIC. The OIC dislikes the Universal Declaration of Human Rights for the very good reason that religion, not excluding their version of it, is a systematic violator of human rights, not least the rights of women—who are one half of the world, a fact the OIC does not notice, or if it does it applies religious arithmetic to solve the problem: One woman is worth half a man. The OIC is trying to change the Universal Declaration of Human Rights accordingly.

"The OIC dislikes the Universal Declaration of Human Rights for the very good reason that religion . . . is a systematic violator of human rights, not least the rights of women."

It has introduced its own version of "(Hu)Man Rights": It is an instructive read, and illustrates the importance of abating the nuisance of religion in today's world. How is this to be done consistently with the right to believe stupid things? By entrenching, and making effective, the principle that whereas you can believe as many stupid things as you like, you are not free to act on those beliefs in ways that harm others.

Danish Freedom of Expression Causes Global Political Unrest

Global Agenda

In the following viewpoint, the editors of Global Agenda *trace the implications of a Danish newspaper's 2005 decision to publish cartoons depicting the prophet Muhammad. Muslims find any representation of the prophet offensive, and the cartoons set off protests and riots around the world. At odds, according to* Global Agenda, *is the right to freedom of expression and the potential harm caused by religious defamation. In many European countries, including Britain, governments are struggling to provide protection for both speech and religion.* Global Agenda *is a publication of the World Economic Forum.*

As you read, consider the following questions:

1. How was the prophet Muhammad depicted in each of the three controversial cartoons, according to the viewpoint?

2. What are the classic Danish food exports, according to the viewpoint?

3. What does the publishing experiment by *Jyllands-Posten* show, according to the writers of this viewpoint?

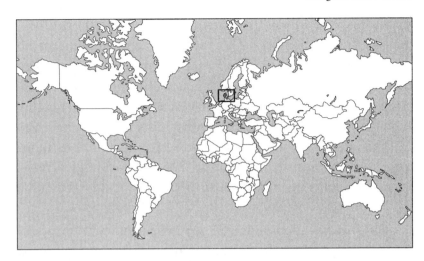

A diplomatic and trade row is raging after several European newspapers—and a Jordanian tabloid—published cartoons of the prophet Muhammad that were deemed insulting by many Muslims. In Britain, meanwhile, parliamentarians have defeated a government proposal to extend laws against incitement to religious hatred. Western democracies are again struggling to reconcile the right to free expression with respect for religious belief.

If the aim was to provoke a reasoned debate about self-censorship, religious intolerance and the freedom of speech, the editors of *Jyllands-Posten* failed miserably. Last September Denmark's biggest selling daily broadsheet noted that a local author could not find artists to illustrate his book about Muhammad. So the paper published a series of cartoons depicting the prophet in various guises, along with an article arguing that "self-censorship . . . rules large parts of the western world". Though the editors said they were "quietly" making their opinion known, the response has been tumultuous.

Any visual representations of the prophet are frowned upon by the faithful. And *Jyllands-Posten*'s cartoons were undeniably strong stuff: one showed Muhammad in bomb-shaped headgear, another depicted him wielding a cutlass and a third had him saying that paradise was running short of virgins for suicide-bombers. The paper insisted that it meant no offence and refused to say sorry. But the pressure on it continued to grow, and on Monday January 30th its editors apologised for any upset they may have caused, while defending their right to publish the cartoons. This did little to calm Muslims in Europe and beyond, who have held protests reminiscent of the frenzied reaction to *The Satanic Verses*, a novel by Salman Rushdie published in 1989. Two of the cartoonists have received death threats.

On Tuesday, thousands of Palestinians gathered for a second day of protests in Gaza, chanting "War on Denmark, death to Denmark" with some burning the Danish flag. On Monday and Thursday, gunmen surrounded the European Union's office in Gaza demanding an apology from the Danish government. Middle Eastern governments and Islamic international organisations, after months of mild grumbling, are now queuing up to berate the Danes. Both Libya and Saudi Arabia have withdrawn their ambassadors from Copenhagen, Denmark's capital. The Danish prime minister, Anders Fogh Rasmussen, points out he is not responsible for what an independent newspaper publishes, though on Tuesday he expressed his personal "distress" that the drawings have been seen by many Muslims "as a defamation of the Prophet Muhammad and Islam as a religion".

That limited apology did not put an end to the controversy. This week an insurgent group in Iraq—where Denmark has 530 troops—said it would target Danes and Norwegians (as a Norwegian newspaper reprinted the cartoons early this year) in retaliation. The al-Aqsa Martyrs' Brigade, the military wing of the Fatah political movement in Gaza and the West Bank, is also threatening to attack Nordic citizens. Nordic aid workers are withdrawing from programmes in Yemen, Gaza and other parts of the Middle East. Denmark has warned its citizens not to travel to Saudi Arabia.

Worse, the row has spread. On Wednesday a French newspaper, *France Soir*, reprinted the Danish cartoons along with drawings of Buddha and Christian and Jewish gods. Its editor declared that "no religious dogma can impose its view on a democratic and secular society . . . we will never apologise for being free to speak, to think and to believe." Representatives of France's 5m-strong Muslim community called the newspaper's decision "appalling" and "a real provocation". The editor was promptly sacked. Across Europe other publications printed the cartoons, which were also published on the Internet. On Thursday, a newspaper in Jordan called on Muslims to "be reasonable" and published three of the offending cartoons.

Religious leaders in the Arab world are in no mood for conciliation, however, and have called for boycotts of Danish products. Across the Gulf and in north Africa supermarkets have withdrawn Scandinavian products from their shelves after customers complained. Arla Foods, a Danish-Swedish dairy producer, says a boycott of its goods has begun, despite its placing advertisements in Middle Eastern newspapers distancing itself from the publication of the cartoons. Though classic Danish food exports—beer and bacon—are not much appreciated in the Middle East, Arla's annual sales in the region are worth $487m. European leaders are lining up to back Denmark. Peter Mandelson, the EU trade commissioner, says Saudi Arabia's government could be hauled before the World Trade Organization if it is thought to be encouraging the boycott of Danish goods.

The clash may also hurt the foreign-policy efforts of Nordic countries more broadly. For years Norway and Sweden, in particular, have been able to pose as peacebrokers, helping to resolve diverse conflicts in Sri Lanka, parts of Africa and in the Middle East. Most notably, Norway hosted peace talks between Israelis and Palestinians in 1993, in Oslo, while recognised as a neutral and disinterested party. Islamic hostility to the Nordic region may make such interventions more difficult in the future.

Locations of Demonstrations, Protests, and Riots in the
Aftermath of the Publication of Caricatures of
Muhammad, Published by Danish Newspaper
Jyllands-Posten in September 2005

Alger, Algeria	Fujairah, United Arab Emirates
Ankara, Turkey	Gallup, New Mexico, USA
Bagram, Afghanistan	Gaza Strip, Palestine
Bangkok, Thailand	Hebron, West Bank
Beirut, Lebanon	Islamabad, Pakistan
Benghazi, Libya	Istanbul, Turkey
Berlin, Germany	Jakarta, Indonesia
Berne, Switzerland	Jalalabad, Afghanistan
Bhopal, India	Jerusalem, Israel
Borno Province, Nigeria	Kabul, Afghanistan
Bossasso, Somalia	Karachi, Pakistan
Cairo, Egypt	Kashmir, India and Pakistan
Cape Town, South Africa	Muzaffarabad, Pakistan
Charikar, Afghanistan	Nablus, West Bank
Chittagong, Bangladesh	Nairobi, Kenya
Copenhagen, Denmark	Nazareth, Israel
Cotabato, Philippines	New Delhi, India
Dacca, Bangladesh	New York, USA
Damascus, Syria	Paris, France
Diyarbakir, Turkey	Peshawar, Pakistan
Djibouti, Djibouti	South Iraq
Dusseldorf, Germany	Strasbourg, France
Faryab, Afghanistan	Sukkur, Pakistan

TAKEN FROM: Compiled by editor.

Back to the Drawing Board

The row also illustrates anew how the right to free expression
in liberal democracies frequently clashes with the sensitivities
of the religious, particularly Muslims. In August last year a
Copenhagen radio station lost its broadcasting licence after a
presenter appeared to call for the extermination of Muslim
migrants. In Italy an anti-Muslim author, Oriana Fallaci, has

launched diatribes against Islam. In November 2004 Theo van Gogh, a Dutch filmmaker and outspoken critic of Islam . . . was murdered by an Islamic extremist.

Former American president Bill Clinton worries that anti-Islamic prejudice is becoming prevalent in western countries. He has also condemned "those totally outrageous cartoons against Islam". But it is unclear how democracies can discourage conflict without clamping down on free expression of opinion. This week Britain's Parliament returned to a debate on extending laws that forbid incitement to religious hatred. Current British law provides limited protection against those who speak out against Jews and Sikhs, but not against those who lambast Christians, Muslims or other believers. The government wanted to change this. It also wanted to curb extremist preachers who urge their followers to commit violence in the name of religion.

"The right to free expression in liberal democracies frequently clashes with the sensitivities of the religious, particularly Muslims."

Yet civil liberties campaigners said anything that limits freedom of expression is undemocratic and that existing laws (in Britain, at least) were sufficient for outlawing incitement to violence. The House of Lords, Parliament's upper chamber, amended the law under debate to ensure firmer defence of freedom of speech. In the Commons, the lower house, the government tried to toughen the bill again to ensure that followers of all faiths are protected against threatening, abusive or insulting behaviour. But the government was defeated in the Commons on Tuesday evening—only the second time it has lost a vote in the lower house since Tony Blair became prime minister in 1997. The Lords' version of the bill, offering greater protection for free expression, triumphed.

Is there at least the possibility of sober debate? The publishing experiment by the editors of *Jyllands-Posten*, whether well-meant or not, shows that calm, rational discussion of the issue is difficult to achieve. And just as it took many years for the controversy over Mr. Rushdie's novel to fade away, this row will long splutter on too.

In Israel, the Constitutional Rights of Freedom of Speech and Religion Must Be Protected

Mike Decker

In the following viewpoint, Mike Decker addresses proposed changes in Israeli laws that would make it illegal to persuade someone to change their religion. He argues that these laws would be an infringement on the right of free speech, and would place Israel in violation of international treaties that the nation has signed. In addition, such laws would also be in opposition to a long-standing legal ruling that any adult may change religion. He concludes that draft laws must be submitted to ensure both freedom of religion and freedom of speech. Decker is a senior legal activist at the Jerusalem Institute of Justice.

As you read, consider the following questions:

1. What U.S. court ruling does Decker cite as an example of the court's support for the freedom of religion and the freedom of speech?

2. What sections of the Israeli criminal law deal with religious persuasion and limit the freedom of religion, according to Decker?

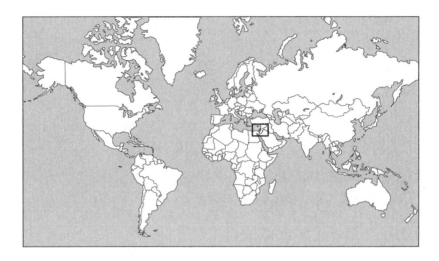

3. Why does Decker think that one of the sections of Israeli criminal law is unbalanced and problematic?

Beginning from the year 2002 and until today [August 7, 2007], there have been in Israel 11 private draft laws submitted, amending two sections of the criminal law. These draft laws decree that any persuasion made to change a person's religion would be considered a criminal offence. Furthermore, advertisements of any sort that have persuasive motives to change people's religion—from a leaflet up to a Web site—would be considered a criminal offence. These draft laws also expand the sanctions which already exist in the criminal law.

Freedom of Speech and Freedom of Religion

They may seem unreasonable in a democratic nation that believes in freedom of speech and freedom of religion. In the United States, for example, religious persuasion is a right protected by the First Amendment of the Constitution which promises that Congress shall not prohibit the free exercise of religion, or abridge the freedom of speech, of the press, or the right of the people to peaceably assemble. Therefore, in the event wherein two rights interconnect, the freedom of speech and religion will almost always overrule. For example, in the famous court ruling wherein it was forbidden for the Jews for Jesus organization to distribute religious leaflets in the airport, *Board of Airport Commissioners of the City of Los Angeles v. Jews for Jesus* (1993), the U.S. Supreme Court viewed the airport's management decision as an unconstitutional decision and therefore void.

The nation of Israel views the freedom of religion as an important value which has already been determined in the Israeli Declaration of Independence wherein it is indicated that the Israeli nation will grant equal civil rights to all its citizens without indifference of religion, gender and sex. The nation of Israel has also signed and ratified international treaties which declare that "everyone shall have the right to freedom of thought, conscience and religion. This right shall include freedom to have or to adopt a religion or belief of his choice, and freedom either individually or in community with others and in public or private, to manifest his religion or belief in worship, observance, practice and teaching". These treaties determine, however, that the freedom to manifest one's religion or beliefs may be subject only to such limitations as are prescribed by law and are necessary to protect public safety, order, health, morals or the fundamental rights and freedoms of others.

"The nation of Israel views the freedom of religion as an important value which has already been determined in the Israeli Declaration of Independence."

Does Israeli Criminal Law Support Freedom of Religion?

In light of the above, I will endeavour to examine whether or not the two existing sections in the Israeli criminal law, which limit the freedom of religion, correspond with the democratic nature of the Israeli nation. As indicated hereinabove, there are two existing sections in the criminal law that deal with religious persuasion and that limit the freedom of religion: sections 174 and 368. Even though, no one was ever convicted of these crimes, the first section determines different criminal sanctions for anyone who conducts a religious ceremony of conversion to a minor which stands in opposition to the law, and to anyone who directly persuades a minor to change his religion. The second section determines that anyone who grants or receives a benefit in courtesy of or as a reward for a religious conversion is considered criminally offensive.

An incident occurred in the *Beit El Mission v. the Minister of Welfare* in the year 1967 regarding the first section of the criminal law that prohibits religious persuasion to minors. This decision dealt with an evangelical Christian organization that requested to establish an orphanage for children of all religions and then train them according to the Christian faith. The minister of welfare prohibited to licence such an orphanage even if both parents of such a child that are not Christian gave their approval. In his court decision Justice Cohen emphasized that freedom of religious expression exists in Israel, however, this right is limited as it relates to minors. In his words—'There is no doubt that just as any person in Israel, regardless of his religion, has the right to change his religion, so does every person have the right to distribute and preach his religion in public in any legal way that he desires—including by way of teaching. However, this is only relevant as it relates to a qualified adult that has the ability to consider the different religious beliefs. On the other hand, a person who is not able to weigh the different religions one against the other because he is a minor or because of some defect, is not able and therefore is not entitled to convert from one religion to another.' Furthermore, Justice Cohen indicates that the Israeli legislator is secular and therefore the concern for the child has to be viewed by secular motives only, and that the issues which pertain to the afterlife are not legitimate claims in the Israeli courts. Such a ruling is obviously difficult for those who believe in the afterlife and obviously for such a believer, the consideration of the afterlife will always overrule the secular considerations of the legislator.

No issue has ever been brought before the Israeli courts regarding the second section of the criminal law dealing with different benefits granted in exchange for religious conversion, and therefore it is very difficult to determine which of the values is being protected that necessitates limiting the freedom of religion.

In any case, I will point out that this section appears unbalanced and problematic when the democratic and Jewish State promises and grants many benefits, such as aliya rights [rights concerning Jewish immigration to Israel], tax benefits, benefits regarding ownership of property, etc., to anyone wishing to join the Jewish religion.

"In order to totally extinguish any chance for such draft laws to ever be accepted by the Israeli Knesset, the rights of freedom of speech and freedom of religion must be anchored as a basic law."

Proposed Changes to the Law Will Damage Democracy

Regarding the abovementioned 11 draft laws which were submitted before the Knesset [Israeli legislative body], it is obvious they stand in opposition to the international treaties ratified by the State of Israel and are in opposition to Justice Cohen's decision which determined that any qualified adult has the right and the freedom to change his religion in any legal way. It is not surprising that all these draft laws were initi-

The Declaration of the Establishment of the State of Israel Guarantees Religious Freedom

THE STATE OF ISRAEL will be open for Jewish immigration and for the Ingathering of the Exiles; it will foster the development of the country for the benefit of all its inhabitants; it will be based on freedom, justice and peace as envisaged by the prophets of Israel; it will ensure complete equality of social and political rights to all its inhabitants irrespective of religion, race or sex; it will guarantee freedom of religion, conscience, language, education and culture; it will safeguard the Holy Places of all religions; and it will be faithful to the principles of the Charter of the United Nations.

"Declaration of the State of Israel,"
Israel Ministry of Foreign Affairs, May 14, 1948.
www.mfa.gov.il.

ated by Knesset members from the religious sector, except for one that was submitted by an orthodox Knesset member and a secular Knesset member (Tomi Lapid).

In order to totally extinguish any chance for such draft laws to ever be accepted by the Israeli Knesset, the rights of freedom of speech and freedom of religion must be anchored as a basic law.

Therefore, just as many draft laws infringing freedom of religion and freedom of speech are being submitted by those who are short-sighted and don't seem to care about these important democratic values, many draft laws which anchor freedom of religion and freedom of speech as basic laws must also be submitted by those who respect and cherish these values as important and necessary in a democratic Jewish State.

In Ireland, the Non-Religious Must Have a Political Voice

Patsy McGarry

In the following viewpoint, Patsy McGarry reports that the non-religious have become the largest group in Ireland, after Roman Catholics. McGarry further reports that the Humanist Association of Ireland provides a political voice for the non-religious. McGarry cites humanist Dick Spicer, who argues that "in a secular state, all perspectives can be accommodated." The Humanist Association, according to McGarry, will represent the Irish non-religious in a dialogue on faith being conducted by the Irish government. McGarry is the religious affairs correspondent for the Irish Times.

As you read, consider the following questions:

1. How many people in the Republic of Ireland either did not state their religion or stated they had no religion on the 2006 census, according to the viewpoint?

2. What does humanist Dick Spicer think might be a "useful social experiment," according to Patsy McGarry?

3. Who is Bertie Ahern, according to the viewpoint?

Dick Spicer, of the Humanist Association of Ireland, believes that in the secular state all perspectives can be accommodated. . . .

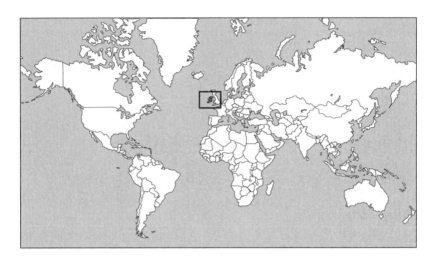

They are the largest "faith" group in the Republic after Catholics—but few of them seem to be aware of it.

An Increase in the Non-Religious

They are, in short, those who ticked the "No Religion" box in the 2006 census form. As many as 186,300 did so, meaning there are more people of no religion in the Republic than there are Church of Ireland members (125,600), Presbyterians (23,500), Orthodox Christians (20,800) and Methodists (12,200) combined.

> *There are more people of no religion in the Republic of Ireland than there are Church of Ireland members, Presbyterians, Orthodox Christians and Methodists combined.*

The census showed there was an increase in the number of such people of 34.6 percent, or 48,000, in 2002. A further 70,300 people did not state their religion in the 2006 census, bringing the total for those in the Republic with "no religion" and who did not state their religion to 256,600 in 2006.

In Northern Ireland the situation is not dissimilar. In the 1991 census, 59,234 people there stated they had "no religion"—3.7 percent of the population. In that same year, 114,827—7.3 percent—did not state their religion. This meant that 174,061, or 11 percent, of the Northern Irish population described themselves as having "no religion" or did not state their religion.

By the time of the 2001 census in Northern Ireland that figure had increased significantly. The numbers of those with "no religion" and those who did not state their religion stood at 233,853, or 13.88 percent of the population.

Insofar as this disparate group of non-believers, agnostics and atheists in either jurisdiction could be said to have a representative voice, it would be through a humanist organisation.

The closest thing to this is the Humanist Association of Ireland in the Republic and the Humanist Association of Northern Ireland.

Last March, both came together to publish *Humanism Ireland* magazine, which plans to appear every two months.

Accommodating All Perspectives

One of the founding members and current vice-chairman of the Humanist Association of Ireland is Dick Spicer. He would not describe himself as an "aggressive secularist". Rather, he believes that "in the secular state all perspectives can be accommodated".

> *"Increasingly people recognize that the way to accommodate diversity is to have mutual State institutions where people can relate without feeling dominated. This allows each group to hold its own perspective."*

He has no problem, for instance, with denominational or multi-denominational schools, but he does believe that where

Religious Affiliation in Ireland

Religion Year	Total	Roman Catholic	Church of Ireland (incl. Protestant)	Presbyterian	Methodist	Jewish	Other Stated Religions	No Religion	Not Stated
1881	3,870,020	3,465,332	317,576	56,498	17,660	394	12,560	—	—
1891	3,468,694	3,099,003	286,804	51,469	18,513	1,506	11,399	—	—
1901	3,221,823	2,878,271	264,264	46,714	17,872	3,006	11,696	—	—
1911	3,139,688	2,812,509	249,535	45,486	16,440	3,805	11,913	—	—
1926	2,971,992	2,751,269	164,215	32,429	10,663	3,686	9,730	—	—
1936	2,968,420	2,773,920	145,030	28,067	9,649	3,749	8,005	—	—
1946	2,955,107	2,786,033	124,829	23,870	8,355	3,907	8,113	—	—
1961	2,818,341	2,673,473	104,016	18,953	6,676	3,255	5,236	1,107	5,625
1971	2,978,248	2,795,666	97,739	16,052	5,646	2,633	6,248	7,616	46,648
1981	3,443,405	3,204,476	95,366	14,255	5,790	2,127	10,843	39,572	70,976
1991	3,525,719	3,228,327	89,187	13,199	5,037	1,581	38,743	66,270	83,375
2002	3,917,203	3,462,606	115,611	20,582	10,033	1,790	89,223	138,264	79,094
2006	4,239,848	3,681,446	125,585	23,546	12,160	1,930	138,541	186,318	70,322

TAKEN FROM: Central Statistics Office (Ireland), 2006 Census. www.cso.ie.

geography disallows choice (e.g. there is just one school in an area), "the school should be persuaded and encouraged towards a more neutral ethos. I don't mean ethically free. We all share similar ethics. We just differ on what we adhere to—humanists to human thought, logic, emotion; religious believers to the divine".

But, he continued, "we can share many perspectives. Religious/denominational education is a positive, at the end of the day". He believes "the secular way of life has become almost the norm in Ireland today" and that "increasingly people recognize that the way to accommodate diversity is to have mutual State institutions where people can relate without feeling dominated. This allows each group to hold its own perspective".

The Breakdown of the Social Structure

As with representatives of faith groups, he too is deeply concerned with what is happening in urban Ireland. He traces the social breakdown in parts of our cities to poor parenting and in many cases to a breakdown in discipline and self-discipline.

Much of this, he said, originated in "so much Irish reliance on the church for ethics and moral guidance. When that was undermined, people were left with nothing. The baby was thrown out with the bathwater".

People lived by "rules from above rather than from an ethical perspective [they had worked out themselves]. They were 'taught' what was 'readymade'. People were told to accept. They were not encouraged to think about what was right", he said.

He criticises the situation whereby "the moral or ethical outlook was dependent on absurdities such as eternal damnation—a system of rewards and punishments".

Such an outlook "should be based on what is rationally right for the human being, for a good life and civil order, rather than on reward and punishment".

People now seem less connected to the local community than in the past and, if not connected in that broader sense, they revert to the tribe or gang, as is evident, he says.

He believes that "many working-class estates have been abandoned to criminals" by the middle classes and he suggested, as a probably useful social experiment, that members of the legal profession ought to be forced to live in those working-class estates and to share in the wreckage caused by drug-addiction, fear and violence.

"We do need direct social constraint. When that goes, it is a recipe for social disorder," he says. "People are not always full of the milk of human kindness. I believe the leniency of the legal system has not helped."

But there are no easy answers. He himself has two sons and, at a time when the family was living in a difficult area, they joined the Defence Forces [Irish military]. "It made them men," he said.

He also believes that an over-emphasis in our education system on the academic has played its part in alienating disaffected young people. He refers to the German system in which the academic and technical are encouraged side by side and enjoy equal status. This means that young people who are more technically minded have other ways of securing self-respect and esteem.

Humanists Will Represent the Non-Religious

He is very happy that the Humanist Association of Ireland has been accepted by the Government as a representative body to take part in the structured dialogue with churches, faith communities and non-confessional bodies. . . .

The structured dialogue had its origins in the original EU [European Union] constitution, finalised under the 2004 Irish presidency of the EU, and it has been incorporated into the Lisbon Treaty [a 2007 agreement about the rights and duties of European member states]. To date, Ireland is the only EU country to have set up the dialogue.

Mr. Spicer says that "to give [Irish prime minister, or "Taoiseach"] Bertie Ahern his due, he was one of the few European leaders whose commitment to such a dialogue was serious. I would like to give him credit for that. He deserves it. I believe he is genuinely religious himself, but he takes other people's perspectives seriously".

In Nigeria, Religion and State Should Be Separated

Eze Enyeribe Onuoha

In the following viewpoint, Eze Enyeribe Onuoha traces the intermingling of state and religion in the nation of Nigeria, detailing the history since colonial days in the nineteenth century. He argues that both Christians and Muslims use unethical and inappropriate means in their attempts to make their faiths the national religion. Onuoha asserts that the Nigerian constitution must be rewritten to ensure that the country is a secular state where people enjoy freedom of both speech and religion. Onuoha is a leader of the Nigerian Humanist Association and the traditional elected head of the Umuchieze people.

As you read, consider the following questions:

1. Who was the first colonial governor of Nigeria?

2. What section of the Nigerian constitution gave Muslims something they wanted, and what section offered Christians something they wanted, according to Eze Enyeribe Onuoha?

3. According to Onuoha, why is the constitution of Nigeria in contradiction with itself?

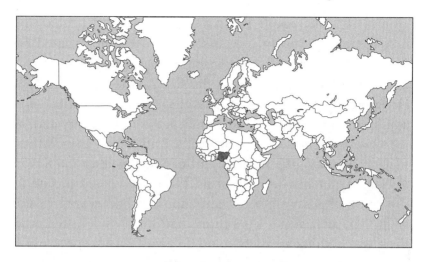

Nigeria is one of the most religious and superstitious countries in the world, frequently troubled by religious strife. There have been many misadventures in relations between Religion and State in the country over the years and in different federal provinces. . . .

The History of Nigerian Religion and State Separation

As to the relations between Religion and State, Nigeria began in 1804 on the wrong foot, with their Union! This negation of Separation was ushered in by a Fulani Muslim scholar, Shaikh Usman dan Fodio, who organized a formidable army of foot-soldiers and horsemen which successfully overran the greater part of Northern Nigeria at the beginning of the 19th century. He imposed on the conquered Hausa peoples of the North "the purity" of the Islamic religion based on a theocracy known as the Sokoto Caliphate. The full Sharia law from the Koran became the law of the land from which there could be no appeal since it was the "Law of God".

This was the situation in 1900 when the British government, in turn, overran both Northern and Southern Nigeria with superior military force and imposed on them a Pax Britannica [British Peace]. The government of Lord Lugard, the first colonial governor, was a secular government based on British law, which was quite incompatible with the crude penal code of the 8th century Sharia. To the dismay of the Hausa-Fulani Muslim ruling class, the "holy law of God" was adjudged repugnant to good conscience and humanity and, as such, was superseded by man-made British law! In addition, religion was abruptly separated from State. Neither the Sultan of Sokoto nor his field marshals, the Emirs, could dictate to the colonial government. The pendulum had swung to the right. The thesis of "Separation" had been established, and there was nothing anybody could do about it—except to nurse a grudge and wait for the end of colonial rule.

"As to the relations between Religion and State, Nigeria began in 1804 on the wrong foot, with their Union!"

Nigerian Independence

Independence came in 1960 and Sir Ahmadu Bello became the Premier of the Northern Region. He sought to be both a political leader and a religious leader. He did not scruple to use the funds and apparatus of government to establish Islamic organizations such as the Jama'atu Nasril Islam (JNI), to convert pagans to Islam and to forge links with Islamic countries across the world. His aspiration to Islamise the nation was rudely interrupted by Nigeria's first military coup d'état on 15th January, 1966, in which, sadly, he was assassinated.

After the Nigerian Civil War, 1966-69, the Head of State, General Yakubu Gowon, though a Christian, was pressured in 1970 by the Kaduna Mafia to expel all foreign missionaries in the East and take over all Mission schools and hospitals in the country, in reprisal for the support given by the Church to the secessionist state of Biafra. In 1975 a Pilgrims Board funded by the State for the exclusive use of Muslims was established.

The Return of Civilian Rule

The return of the country to civilian rule in 1979 provided the Muslim elite in the North with another opportunity to breach the Separation principle. The new opportunity was the Constituent Assembly set up by the out-going [Olusegun] Obasanjo military government in 1977 to draft a new Constitution for the nation. What could be better than to inscribe the Muslim theocratic legal system right into the Constitution? The Sharia law debate that ensued was long, loud and bitter. The Assembly was sharply divided between Christians striving to maintain the secularity of the State and Muslims bent on the Islamization of the nation. At a point in the debate, the Muslims actually staged a walkout!

At the end, the Muslims got, in Section 275, a Sharia Court of Appeal (subject, however, to the Supreme Court) while the Christians got Section 10, curtly and rather vaguely stating that "the government of the federation or of a State shall not adopt any religion as State Religion", in other words, that Nigeria is, de jure [concerning law], a secular State. But, by this compromise, the Constitution contradicted itself. Sections 10 and 275 are, patently, in mutual contradiction.

"The [Nigerian] Assembly was sharply divided between Christians striving to maintain the secularity of the State and Muslims bent on the Islamization of the nation."

The Second Nigerian Republic

The Second Republic came on stream in 1979 under President Shehu Shagari. Unable to restrain himself from active participation in the promotion of religion, he adopted the "balancing act strategy". He would do one favour to Muslims and balance it with another for Christians. Thus, in 1980, he established a Christian Pilgrims Board to make up for the existing Muslim Pilgrims Board. In 1982, he established a Board

Religion in Nigeria: Statistics

Religion	Percentage of Population
Islam	50%
Roman Catholic	14%
Protestant	26%
Indigenous Beliefs	10%

"Nigerian Religion Stats," NationMaster.com, June 7, 2009. www.nationmaster.com.

for Islamic Affairs. He built two mosques and one Id-el-Fitri Muslim Praying Ground in Abuja, the State Capital, and, in compensation, donated ten million naira to Christians to enable them build their own Cathedral. (The Christians used the money to build a Christian Ecumenical Centre at Abuja, instead).

While the President was doing this on the official level, at public expense, from 1980 Muslims in the North resorted to another strategy at the informal, unofficial level: the use of localized physical force and religious riots to protest against the failure of Nigeria to adopt Islam as the national religion. Between 1980 and 1992, a researcher recorded 25 such riots in which innocent people were killed or maimed, churches and houses burned, and shops looted.

In 1986, the military President, Ibrahim Babangida, employing all his powers as a dictator, registered Nigeria as a full member of the Organisation of the Islamic Conference.

Muslim Strategy

We can count six ways in which Muslims in Nigeria have striven to Islamise the country:

1. All-out war: a holy war or jihad; conversion by the sword, with the establishment of a Caliphate [the dominion of a Caliph, a spiritual head of Islam] as the ultimate objective.

2. Politicians doubling as religious leaders. Abuse of political office: State financing of religion on the principle of cuius regio, eius religio ["in a prince's country, the prince's religion"].

3. Military takeover of government; suspending the Constitution and installing a Muslim Military Head of State.

4. Getting the Sharia inscribed in the Constitution.

5. Constant religious riots, bloodshed and destruction of property organized by a mafia to pressurize the sitting President.

6. Lastly, breaking the Constitution in open defiance of the Federal Government, threatening a Civil War. "Islam shall be the State religion, or else. . ."

This last technique, with the threat of a civil war, has recently been successfully used in Nigeria in opposition to President Olusegun Obasanjo.

In 2000, the governor of Zamfara State, Ahmed Sani Yerima, launched with fanfare the introduction of the Sharia Penal Code in Zamfara State, one of the 36 States of Nigeria. In effect, Zamfara became a holy State reminiscent of the Holy Roman Empire of blessed memory. This meant that beer could no longer be sold in restaurants, boys and girls could not hold hands in the street or sit together in a bus, a Muslim girl cannot marry a Christian boy, a Muslim cannot convert to another religion without incurring apostasy [a rejection of and formal disaffiliation of one's religion], a woman caught in adultery will be stoned to death, a man will have his hand cut off for stealing, etc.—according to the holy law of their tyrannical God.

The whole country held its breath, watching to see what the President would do. For a whole month, the governor of Zamfara and the President of Nigeria were staring at each other, eyeball to eyeball. In the end, it was the President who blinked first. Immediately, eleven other States in the Muslim North joined Zamfara and installed the Sharia: Zamfara, Yobe, Taraba, Sokoto, Kebbi, Katsina, Kano, Kaduna, Jigawa, Gombe, Bauchi and Niger States. The President chose peace with a battered Constitution rather than be drawn into another civil war!

Christian Strategy

The Christians, for their part, habitually use the second technique, abuse of power, to infiltrate government institutions, public mass media, schools and hospitals employing them corruptly as means of evangelization. They do this wherever they are the dominant population. They conduct religious services, preach their sermons and work their miracles on State radio and television, in hospitals, and even in government ministries during morning assemblies. In some States, at 12:00 noon every day, the Angelus [a Christian prayer] is recited triumphantly on State radio.

Religion gets more airtime than agriculture, health, science and technology!

"Whether carried out by the Nigerian government or by the messianic religions (Christianity and Islam), the mixing of Religion and State is morally wrong."

Christians had long ago, during the colonial era, imposed their religious holidays on the entire nation. It was the flaunting of Christianity during the colonial era that provoked the Muslim backlash after Independence, as a result of which Nigeria, today, has far too many religious holidays. The Church should impose its holidays on its own members, not on the entire nation. In the days before the Biafran War, Nigerian governments were subsidizing Christian and Islamic schools, calling them "government-aided schools". In effect, government was subsidizing evangelism: something it should never do.

The Mixing of Religion and State Must Be Stopped

Whether carried out by the Nigerian government or by the messianic religions (Christianity and Islam), the mixing of Religion and State is morally wrong. It is an offence against freedom of thought and conscience of Nigerian citizens, many of whom are unbelievers—a freedom enshrined in Section 38 of the Constitution. A Constitution that makes Nigeria a secular State and at the same time makes room for a Sharia Court of Appeal is in contradiction with itself.

Section 10 of the Nigerian Constitution, titled "Prohibition of State Religion", which has now become a dead law, must be revived. The way to do so is to subject that Section to further clarification by means of subsections, which state clearly, with the benefit of hindsight, what can, or cannot, be done under the Section. We propose seven subsections:

- Subsection (1)—That no government in Nigeria, Federal, State or Local, shall fund religion or religious activities in any way.

- Subsection (2)—No government in Nigeria shall affiliate in a religious organization, within or outside, the nation.

- Subsection (3)—No government in Nigeria shall adopt a law peculiar to any religion.

- Subsection (4)—No government in Nigeria shall participate officially in religious services, activities or programmes, or adopt religious names, images or symbols nor participate in the selection, appointment or installation of religious authorities.

- Subsection (5)—Religion shall not be taught, and proselytizing shall not be practised, in public schools, hospitals, and institutions.

- Subsection (6)—The State shall not take over property belonging to religious organizations without paying adequate compensation.

- Subsection (7)—Any State that breaches Section 10 of the Constitution shall be deemed to have withdrawn from the Federation and, therefore, shall, after due process, be denied Federal allocation of funds until it purges itself of its effrontery.

With Section 10 thus elaborated, Nigeria will become truly a secular State: that is, a State whose responsibility is limited to the mundane, that is, to the promotion of the security and physical welfare of its people, a State where religion is clearly in the private domain even where it is the religion of the majority, or the religion of the President or Governor, a State where religion, irreligion and State can co-exist and develop separately and peacefully, a State where freedom of conscience is the inalienable right of everyone.

Periodical Bibliography

The following articles have been selected to supplement the diverse views presented in this chapter.

Vishal Arora "Religion and Politics in India," The Oxford Centre for Religion in Public Life, August 1, 2008. www.crpl.org.

Michael Charney "Buddha's Irresistible Maroon Army," *Times*, December 15, 2007.

Johann Hari "When Two Sides of Islam Go Head to Head," *Independent*, June 23, 2008.

Philip Jenkins "When Jesus Met Buddha," *Boston Globe*, December 14, 2008.

Martin Kay "Faithful Gather to Foster Unity and Tolerance: Interfaith Dialogue Seen as Tool in Fight Against Global Terrorism," *Dominion Post*, May 28, 2007.

Joseph Loconte "The New Fundamentalists: Media Gatekeepers," *Weekly Standard*, December 20, 2007.

John Micklethwait "The Culture Wars Go Global," *Economist*, November 15, 2007.

Clarissa Oon "Politicization of Buddhism? Monks Marching for Faith and Justice," *Straits Times*, March 24, 2008.

John T. Sidel "The New Trinity: Religion, Knowledge and Power," *Straits Times*, October 24, 2007.

Margaret Somerville "The Search for a Shared Ethics: All Voices, Religious and Secular, Have a Right to Be Heard in Societal Debates," *Globe and Mail*, January 27, 2009.

 **GLOBAL**VIEWPOINTS

CHAPTER 4

Religion and Violence

Tibetan Buddhists Claim Oppression from China

His Holiness the 14th Dalai Lama

In the following viewpoint, His Holiness the 14th Dalai Lama, the spiritual leader of the Tibetan people, traces the history of the Chinese occupation of Tibet, noting that since the 1950s, the Chinese have engaged in oppressive and sometimes violent actions in Tibet. He argues that Tibetans fear the Chinese and that their religion and culture are being destroyed. Since March 2008, the situation has worsened, according to the Dalai Lama, with a Chinese crackdown on Tibetan protests and a propaganda campaign against the leadership of the Dalai Lama. He urges Tibetans to continue the "path of truth and nonviolence."

As you read, consider the following questions:

1. To where did nearly a hundred thousand Tibetans flee in 1959, according to His Holiness the 14th Dalai Lama?

2. What Chinese leader asked for Tibetan forgiveness from the Tibetans in 1980?

3. According to the Dalai Lama, what is his aspiration for all Tibetans?

Today [March 9, 2009] is the fiftieth anniversary of the Tibetan people's peaceful uprising against Communist China's repression in Tibet. Since last March widespread peace-

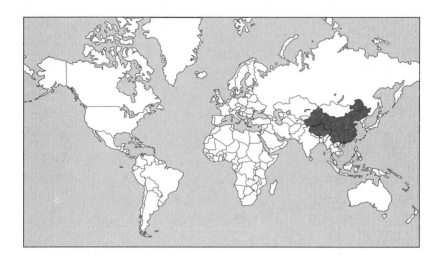

ful protests have erupted across the whole of Tibet. Most of the participants were youths born and brought up after 1959, who have not seen or experienced a free Tibet. However, the fact that they were driven by a firm conviction to serve the cause of Tibet that has continued from generation to generation is indeed a matter of pride. It will serve as a source of inspiration for those in the international community who take keen interest in the issue of Tibet. We pay tribute and offer our prayers for all those who died, were tortured and suffered tremendous hardships, including during the crisis last year, for the cause of Tibet since our struggle began.

The Chinese Communist Occupation of Tibet

Around 1949, Communist forces began to enter northeastern and eastern Tibet (Kham and Amdo) and by 1950, more than 5000 Tibetan soldiers had been killed. Taking the prevailing situation into account, the Chinese government chose a policy of peaceful liberation, which in 1951 led to the signing of the 17-point Agreement and its annexure. Since then, Tibet has come under the control of the People's Republic of China.

However, the Agreement clearly mentions that Tibet's distinct religion, culture and traditional values would be protected.

Between 1954 and 1955, I met with most of the senior Chinese leaders in the Communist Party, government and military, led by Chairman Mao Zedong, in Beijing. When we discussed ways of achieving the social and economic development of Tibet, as well as maintaining Tibet's religious and cultural heritage, Mao Zedong and all the other leaders agreed to establish a preparatory committee to pave the way for the implementation of the autonomous region, as stipulated in the Agreement, rather than establishing a military administrative commission. From about 1956 onwards, however, the situation took a turn for the worse with the imposition of ultra-leftist policies in Tibet. Consequently, the assurances given by higher authorities were not implemented on the ground. The forceful implementation of the so-called "democratic" reforms in the Kham and Amdo regions of Tibet, which did not accord with prevailing conditions, resulted in immense chaos and destruction. In Central Tibet, Chinese officials forcibly and deliberately violated the terms of the 17-point Agreement, and their heavy-handed tactics increased day by day. These desperate developments left the Tibetan people with no alternative but to launch a peaceful uprising on 10 March 1959. The Chinese authorities responded with unprecedented force that led to the killing, arrests and imprisonment of tens of thousands of Tibetans in the following months. Consequently, accompanied by a small party of Tibetan government officials including some Kalons (Cabinet Ministers), I escaped into exile in India. Thereafter, nearly a hundred thousand Tibetans fled into exile in India, Nepal and Bhutan. During the escape and the months that followed they faced unimaginable hardship, which is still fresh in Tibetan memory.

Having occupied Tibet [in the 1950s], the Chinese Communist government carried out a series of repressive and violent campaigns that have included "democratic" reform, class struggle, communes, the Cultural Revolution, the imposition of martial law, and more recently the patriotic re-education and the strike hard campaigns. These thrust Tibetans into such depths of suffering and hardship that they literally experienced hell on earth. The immediate result of these campaigns was the deaths of hundreds of thousands of Tibetans. The lineage of the Buddha Dharma [the Truth pointed out by Buddha] was severed. Thousands of religious and cultural centres such as monasteries, nunneries and temples were razed to the ground. Historical buildings and monuments were demolished. Natural resources have been indiscriminately exploited. Today, Tibet's fragile environment has been polluted, massive deforestation has been carried out and wildlife, such as wild yaks and Tibetan antelopes, are being driven to extinction.

Fifty Years of Suffering for Tibet

These 50 years have brought untold suffering and destruction to the land and people of Tibet. Even today, Tibetans in Tibet live in constant fear and the Chinese authorities remain constantly suspicious of them. Today, the religion, culture, language and identity, which successive generations of Tibetans have considered more precious than their lives, are nearing extinction; in short, the Tibetan people are regarded like criminals deserving to be put to death. The Tibetan people's tragedy was set out in the late Panchen Rinpoche's [the second highest Tibetan spiritual leader] 70,000-character petition to the Chinese government in 1962. He raised it again in his speech in Shigatse [Tibet's second largest city] in 1989 shortly before he died, when he said that what we have lost under Chinese Communist rule far outweighs what we have gained. Many concerned and unbiased Tibetans have also spoken out about the hardships faced by the Tibetan people. Even Hu Yaobang, the Communist Party Secretary, when he arrived in

Lhasa [the capital of the Tibet Autonomous Region] in 1980, clearly acknowledged these mistakes and asked the Tibetans for their forgiveness. Many infrastructural developments such as roads, airports, railways, and so forth, which seem to have brought progress to Tibetan areas, were really done with the political objective of sinicising [to bring under Chinese influence] Tibet at the huge cost of devastating the Tibetan environment and way of life.

As for the Tibetan refugees, although we initially faced many problems such as great differences of climate and language and difficulties earning our livelihood, we have been successful in re-establishing ourselves in exile. Due to the great generosity of our host countries, especially India, Tibetans have been able to live in freedom without fear. We have been able to earn a livelihood and uphold our religion and culture. We have been able to provide our children with both traditional and modern education, as well as engaging in efforts to resolve the Tibet issue. There have been other positive results too. Greater understanding of Tibetan Buddhism with its emphasis on compassion has made a positive contribution in many parts of the world.

"Many infrastructural developments such as roads, airports, railways, and so forth ... were really done with the political objective of sinicising Tibet at the huge cost of devastating the Tibetan environment and way of life."

Immediately after our arrival in exile we began to work on the promotion of democracy in the Tibetan community with the establishment of the Tibetan Parliament-in-Exile in 1960. Since then, we have taken gradual steps on the path to democracy and today our exile administration has evolved into a fully functioning democracy with a written charter of its own and a legislative body. This is indeed something we can all be proud of.

Since 2001, we have instituted a system by which the political leadership of Tibetan exiles is directly elected through procedures similar to those in other democratic systems. Currently, the directly-elected Kalon Tripa's (Cabinet Chairperson) second term is underway. Consequently, my daily administrative responsibilities have reduced and today I am in a state of semi-retirement. However, to work for the just cause of Tibet is the responsibility of every Tibetan, and I will uphold this responsibility.

The Dalai Lama's Commitments

As a human being my main commitment is in the promotion of human values; this is what I consider the key factor for a happy life at the individual level, family level and community level. As a religious practitioner, my second commitment is the promotion of inter-religious harmony. My third commitment is of course the issue of Tibet due to my being a Tibetan with the name of the 'Dalai Lama', but more importantly it is due to the trust that Tibetans both inside and outside Tibet have placed in me. These are the three important commitments, which I always keep in mind.

> *"The Chinese insistence that we accept Tibet as having been a part of China since ancient times is not only inaccurate but unreasonable."*

In addition to looking after the well-being of the exiled Tibetan community, which they have done quite well, the principal task of the Central Tibetan Administration has been to work towards the resolution of the issue of Tibet. Having laid out the mutually beneficial Middle-Way policy in 1974, we were ready to respond to [Chinese leader] Deng Xiaoping when he proposed talks in 1979. Many talks were conducted and fact-finding delegations dispatched. These, however, did not bear any concrete results and formal contacts eventually broke off in 1993.

Subsequently, in 1996-97, we conducted an opinion poll of the Tibetans in exile, and collected suggestions from Tibet wherever possible, on a proposed referendum, by which the Tibetan people were to determine the future course of our freedom struggle to their full satisfaction. Based on the outcome of the poll and the suggestions from Tibet, we decided to continue the policy of the Middle-Way.

Since the re-establishment of contacts in 2002, we have followed a policy of one official channel and one agenda and have held eight rounds of talks with the Chinese authorities. As a consequence, we presented a Memorandum on Genuine Autonomy for the Tibetan People, explaining how the conditions for national regional autonomy as set forth in the Chinese constitution would be met by the full implementation of its laws on autonomy. The Chinese insistence that we accept Tibet as having been a part of China since ancient times is not only inaccurate but also unreasonable. We cannot change the past no matter whether it was good or bad. Distorting history for political purposes is incorrect.

"There has been a brutal crackdown on the Tibetan protests that have shaken the whole of Tibet since March . . . [2008]."

Looking Toward the Future

We need to look to the future and work for our mutual benefit. We Tibetans are looking for a legitimate and meaningful autonomy, an arrangement that would enable Tibetans to live within the framework of the People's Republic of China. Fulfilling the aspirations of the Tibetan people will enable China to achieve stability and unity. From our side, we are not making any demands based on history. Looking back at history, there is no country in the world today, including China, whose territorial status has remained forever unchanged, nor can it remain unchanged.

"China/Tibet," cartoon by Felipe Galindo, CartoonStock.com. Copyright © Felipe Galindo. Reproduction rights obtainable from www.CartoonStock.com.

Our aspiration that all Tibetans be brought under a single autonomous administration is in keeping with the very objective of the principle of national regional autonomy. It also fulfils the fundamental requirements of the Tibetan and Chinese peoples. The Chinese constitution and other related laws and regulations do not pose any obstacle to this and many leaders of the Chinese Central Government have accepted this genuine aspiration. When signing the 17-point Agreement, Premier Zhou Enlai acknowledged it as a reasonable demand. In 1956, when establishing the Preparatory Committee for the Tibet Autonomous Region, Vice-Premier Chen Yi pointing at a map said, if Lhasa could be made the capital of the Tibet Autonomous Region, which included the Tibetan areas within the other provinces, it would contribute to the development of Tibet and friendship between the Tibetan and Chinese nationalities, a view shared by the late Panchen Rinpoche and many educated Tibetans, cadres among them. If Chinese leaders had any objections to our proposals, they could have provided reasons for them and suggested alternatives for our consideration, but they did not. I am disappointed that the Chinese authorities have not responded appropriately to our sincere efforts to implement the principle of meaningful national regional autonomy for all Tibetans, as set forth in the constitution of the People's Republic of China.

Quite apart from the current process of Sino-Tibetan dialogue having achieved no concrete results, there has been a brutal crackdown on the Tibetan protests that have shaken the whole of Tibet since March last year [2008]. Therefore, in order to solicit public opinion as to what future course of action we should take, the Special Meeting of Tibetan exiles was convened in November 2008. Efforts were made to collect suggestions, as far as possible, from the Tibetans in Tibet as well. The outcome of this whole process was that a majority of Tibetans strongly supported the continuation of the Middle-Way policy. Therefore, we are now pursuing this policy with greater confidence and will continue our efforts towards achieving a meaningful national regional autonomy for all Tibetans.

From time immemorial, the Tibetan and Chinese peoples have been neighbours. In future too, we will have to live together. Therefore, it is most important for us to co-exist in friendship with each other.

Chinese Propaganda Distorts the Truth About Tibet

Since the occupation of Tibet, Communist China has been publishing distorted propaganda about Tibet and its people.

Consequently, there are, among the Chinese populace, not many who have a true understanding about Tibet. It is, in fact, very difficult for them to find the truth. There are also ultra-leftist Chinese leaders who have, since last March, been undertaking a huge propaganda effort with the intention of setting the Tibetan and Chinese peoples apart and creating animosity between them. Sadly, as a result, a negative impression of Tibetans has arisen in the minds of some of our Chinese brothers and sisters. Therefore, as I have repeatedly appealed before, I would like once again to urge our Chinese brothers and sisters not to be swayed by such propaganda, but, instead, to try to discover the facts about Tibet impartially, so as to prevent divisions among us. Tibetans should also continue to work for friendship with the Chinese people.

Looking back on 50 years in exile, we have witnessed many ups and downs. However, the fact that the Tibet issue is alive and the international community is taking growing interest in it is indeed an achievement. Seen from this perspective, I have no doubt that the justice of Tibet's cause will prevail, if we continue to tread the path of truth and non-violence.

"There are also ultra-leftist Chinese leaders who have ... been undertaking a huge propaganda effort with the intention of setting the Tibetan and Chinese peoples apart."

As we commemorate 50 years in exile, it is most important that we express our deep gratitude to the governments and peoples of the various host countries in which we live. Not only do we abide by the laws of these host countries, but we also conduct ourselves in a way that we become an asset to these countries. Similarly, in our efforts to realise the cause of Tibet and uphold its religion and culture, we should craft our future vision and strategy by learning from our past experience.

China Claims the Dalai Lama Incites Violence

Lu Hui

In the following viewpoint, China View *editor Lu Hui argues that rather than trying to bring peace to Tibet, the Dalai Lama incites violence. He asserts that since the 1950s, the Dalai Lama's words and his actions are contradictory, demonstrated by his first signing agreements with China and then leaving the country to set up a government in exile. The writer argues that the Dalai Lama is responsible for attempting to sabotage Chinese unity by advocating for an independent Tibet. He concludes that it is the Dalai Lama who is responsible for breaking off dialogue, not the Chinese government.*

As you read, consider the following questions:

1. To what post was the Dalai Lama elected in March 1955, according to the viewpoint?

2. Who passed away in early 1989, according to the viewpoint?

3. What does the writer say the Dalai Lama will have to give up to open the door to dialogue with the Chinese?

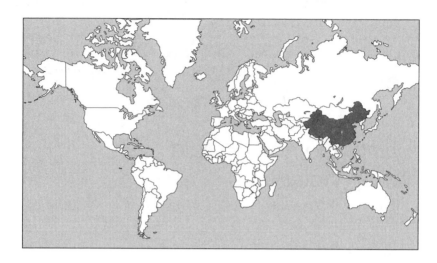

Buddhist precepts tell followers to be good to their word and never lie. The Buddhist Dalai Lama clique, however, seems to have never quite followed these teachings.

On March 14 [2008], violence of riotous beating, looting and arson erupted in Lhasa, capital of the Tibet Autonomous Region in southwest China. The following day, the Dalai Lama said in Dharamshala [a city in northern India, where the Dalai Lama resides] that "these protests are a manifestation of the deep-rooted resentment of the Tibetan people under the present governance."

"The past decades have seen the Dalai Lama clique, a real troublemaker, constantly break its words."

On March 28 [2008], he wrote in a lengthy statement, "Chinese brothers and sisters, I assure you I have no desire to seek Tibet's separation. Nor do I have any wish to drive a wedge between the Tibetan and Chinese peoples."

However, the past decades have seen the Dalai Lama clique, a real troublemaker, constantly break its words.

The Dalai Lama's Words and Deeds Do Not Square

First, examine what the Dalai Lama clique has said and what it has actually done since the 1950s.

In May 1951, representatives of the central government and the Tibet local government signed an agreement on the region's peaceful liberation, widely known as the 17 Pacts.

On Oct. 24, the Dalai Lama telegraphed Chairman Mao Zedong, saying the agreement had won unanimous support from the Tibet local government and the Tibetan people, including monks and civilians.

Besides, the telegraph said, under the leadership of Chairman Mao and the central government, the Tibet local government and people would actively assist the People's Liberation Army in Tibet to consolidate national defense and banish imperialist forces from the region to safeguard the motherland's unity in territory and sovereignty.

In March 1955, the Dalai Lama attended the first session of the National People's Congress (NPC) in Beijing and was elected vice chairman of the NPC standing committee.

Before leaving Beijing, he presented to Chairman Mao a gilded dharma and a gilded picture frame with Mao's picture in it. The bottom part of the frame was engraved in both Tibetan and Chinese with such words as "Beloved Chairman Mao, we will follow you forever in building a new Tibet and building the great motherland."

On Oct. 1, 1958, the Dalai Lama published an article in the *People's Daily*, saying: "The Tibetans are one of the ethnic groups with a long history within the Chinese territory. Since returning to the big family of the motherland, the Tibetan people, together with other ethnic brothers, have fully enjoyed the rights of freedom and equality."

However, merely months later, the Dalai Lama and his backers tore up the agreement on Tibet's peaceful liberation and backed the armed rebellion of the secessionist forces. They fled abroad to form a "Tibetan government-in-exile."

The Recent Record

The Dalai Lama has been trying to build an image that he is eager to talk with the Chinese government but was turned down by the latter. Whether this is the truth or not, we need to revisit the more recent record.

On March 1979, China's late state leader, Deng Xiaoping, met with a private envoy of the Dalai Lama in person. Deng told him: "Tibet is part of China. This is the basic principle and criteria to judge whether the behavior is right or not."

In the following years, the Chinese government received a number of delegations sent by the Dalai Lama, including most of his family members who fled abroad, according to a government source.

Those people spread the word on "Tibet independence" during their journeys to Tibet, undertaken in the name of touring and visiting people.

In the 1980s, the Dalai Lama put forth his "middle course" on Tibet: greater autonomy in so-called "Greater Tibet," which covers a much larger area than the present Tibet.

The two schemes featuring this topic, the "five-point peace plan" he presented to the U.S. Congress in 1987 and the "new seven-point proposal" presented in the hall of the European Parliament in Strasbourg in 1988, did not stray from "Tibet independence" and still advocated that Tibet was an "independent country" in history.

While sparing no effort to mislead the international community, he and his supporters masterminded riots in Lhasa in 1989, joining hands with foreign forces.

In early 1989 when the 10th Panchen Lama, another grand living Buddha of Tibet, passed away, then Chairman of the Buddhist Association of China Zhao Puchu personally handed

Tibet Will Not Be Independent

In an interview with Xinhua News Agency reporters on May 19, 1991, on the eve of the 40th anniversary of Tibet's peaceful liberation, Premier Li Peng of the State Council of the People's Republic of China pointed out, "The central government's policy towards the Dalai Lama has been consistent and remains unchanged. We have only one fundamental principle, namely, Tibet is an inalienable part of China. On this fundamental issue there is no room for haggling. The central government has always expressed its willingness to have contact with the Dalai Lama, but he must stop activities to split the motherland and change his position for 'Tibetan independence.' All matters except 'Tibetan independence' can be discussed."

. . . To be responsible for the history, the Chinese nation and its 1.1 billion people, including the Tibetan people, the central government will make not the slightest concession on the fundamental issue of maintaining the motherland's unification. Any activity attempting to realize "Tibetan independence" and split the motherland by relying on foreign forces is an ignominious move betraying the motherland and the whole Chinese nation including the Tibetan nationality. The central government resolutely denounces this kind of action and will never allow it to succeed. The central government will continue to implement a series of special policies and preferential measures to promote the construction and development of Tibet. . . . Any activity sabotaging stability and unity in Tibet and any unlawful deed creating disturbance and inciting riots runs against the basic interests of the Tibetan people and will be cracked down on relentlessly.

White Papers of the Government,
Information Office of the State Council
of the People's Republic of China, "The Dalai Clique's
Separatist Activities and the Central Government Policy,"
Tibet—Its Ownership and Human Rights Situation,
September 1992. www.china.org.

a letter to the Dalai Lama's private envoy in which he invited the Dalai Lama to return to China for mourning ceremonies.

However, he refused the invitation and missed a valuable chance to talk with the Chinese government face to face, despite having frequently said he was homesick.

During an anti-China whirlwind in the late 1980s and early 1990s, the Dalai Lama and his followers immediately tuned their attitude towards "negotiations with China"—he was in no hurry to talk with the Chinese government that he thought would "collapse" soon.

The Dalai Lama Has Closed the Dialogue with China

Dealing with such a person, who can blow hot and cold, the Chinese government has shown the greatest patience.

At this year's [2008] legislative season Premier Wen Jiabao reiterated that the door of dialogue remains open to the Dalai Lama, so long as he gives up "Tibet independence", stops splitting and sabotaging activities, and recognizes Tibet and Taiwan as inalienable parts of the Chinese territory.

"Dealing with such a person [the Dalai Lama], who can blow hot and cold, the Chinese government has shown the greatest patience."

This week, the Dalai Lama told U.S. media: "The Chinese government wants me to say that for many centuries Tibet has been part of China. Even if I make that statement, many people would just laugh. And my statement will not change past history. History is history."

Yes, history is history. Judging from the history of the 14th Dalai Lama, he just did not act as he said. It was the Dalai Lama clique that closed the door of dialogue.

Iranian Bahá'í
Suffer Persecution

Jonathan Spollen

In the following viewpoint, Jonathan Spollen reports on charges brought against the leadership of the Iranian Bahá'í faith, arguing that the charges and scheduled trial are part of a governmentally sanctioned and systematic persecution of members of the religion. These seven are among 80 others of their faith who are also in prison awaiting trial. He writes further that Bahá'í members have no legal status in Iran, and that they have been discriminated against in jobs and employment. Spollen is the assistant foreign editor at the National, *an English-language newspaper based in the United Arab Emirates.*

As you read, consider the following questions:

1. Where is the location of the prison where the seven defendants are being held, according to Jonathan Spollen?
2. What is the House of Bab, where is it located, and what happened to it, according to the viewpoint?
3. When, where, and by whom was the Bahá'í faith established?

As seven leaders of the Bahá'í faith prepare to go on trial in Iran on charges ranging from spying for Israel to insulting Islam, the case is bringing the plight of the Bahá'í

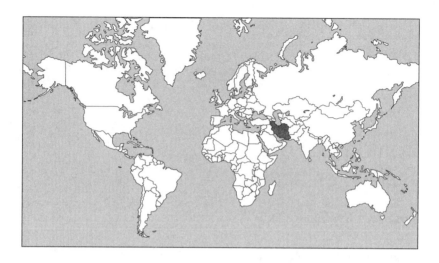

community into the spotlight, underscoring what critics say is years of persecution by the Iranian regime that has begun reaching into the upper ranks of its leadership.

The seven defendants, five men and two women, stand accused of "espionage for Israel, insulting religious sanctities and propaganda against the Islamic republic". But human rights advocates say the charges are baseless and offer all the trappings of a show trial.

They have languished in Evin prison, just north of [the Iranian capital] Tehran, for nearly a year without access to their lawyer, the Nobel Laureate Shirin Ebadi. If found guilty they face a maximum penalty of death.

Human rights advocates say Iranian charges against seven Bahá'í leaders are baseless and offer all the trappings of a show trial.

"They have not had any contact with Ms. Ebadi at all, she has not even had access to their files," said Nazila Ghanea, a lecturer in international human rights law at Oxford University and author of *Human Rights, the UN and the Bahá'ís in Iran*. The situation, she said, was "illegal under Iranian law".

Many Bahá'ís Languish in Prison

Diane Ala'i, the Geneva-based representative to the United Nations for the Bahá'í International Community, said the seven Bahá'ís were targeted because they are leaders of the community in Iran, but said at least 35 other Bahá'ís also languish in prison, while 80 others had been released on bail awaiting trial.

"These people are being held only because they are Bahá'ís," she said.

Several rights groups and organisations have condemned the trial, as have the United Nations, the European Union and the governments of the United States and Britain.

But Iran insists it has "irrefutable evidence" of the individuals' guilt.

"Bahá'í organisations are illegal and their connections to Israel and their enmity toward Islam and the Islamic system are absolutely certain and their threat against the national security is a proven fact," Qorban-Ali Dorri-Najafabadi, Iran's prosecutor general, told the state-run Press TV.

But critics say the trial is just the latest instance in a well-documented record of persecution against the Bahá'ís since the 1979 revolution.

Soon after the establishment of the Islamic republic, dozens of Bahá'í members were arrested and executed, including eight of the community's nine leaders who were hanged without a trial. In the years since, at least 200 have been executed, according to Amnesty International and other rights groups, with many missing and thousands more imprisoned.

Bahá'í groups both in and outside Iran say members living there are systematically denied jobs, pensions and the right to inherit property and say that more than 10,000 have been dismissed from government and university posts since 1979.

Moreover, dozens of Bahá'í buildings, cemeteries and holy sites have been seized and destroyed since the revolution. One of the holiest Bahá'í sites, the House of [the] Báb in Shiraz, was razed and an Islamic centre was built on its ruins.

Prof. Ghanea said the Bahá'í experience in Iran since the revolution amounted to "civil death".

With about 300,000 members, Bahá'ís are the largest religious minority in Iran, but they "have no legal status though they constitute the largest non-Muslim religious minority community", she said. "They are, however, singled out at every opportunity for discrimination and exclusion."

Officially Sanctioned Discrimination

A secret government report drafted by the Iranian Supreme Revolutionary Cultural Council and signed by Supreme Leader Ali Khamenei, and which was uncovered by the UN in 1993, appears to support allegations of officially sanctioned discrimination.

The letter, written in 1991, says the "government's dealings with [the Bahá'ís] must be in such a way that their progress and development are blocked". It recommends that Bahá'ís not be allowed to enrol in schools if they identify themselves as Bahá'ís and calls for their expulsion from universities.

The letter goes on to urge the government to "deny them employment" or "any position of influence, such as in the educational sector".

Indeed, out of those on trial several have lost jobs, businesses or been denied education for their faith.

"Iran's Shiite religious establishment considers the [Bahá'í] religion a heretical offshoot of Islam."

Fariba Kamalabadi, 46, a developmental psychologist, was not allowed to study at a public university; Jamaloddin Khanjani, 75, had his brick-making factory seized in the early 1980s; and Mahvash Sabet, 55, was dismissed from her position as a school principal.

Bahá'ís Are Subjected to Persecution in Iran

Since 1979, Iranian Bahá'ís have faced a government-sponsored, systematic campaign of religious persecution in their homeland. In its early stages, more than 200 Bahá'ís were killed and at least 1,000 were imprisoned, solely because of their religious beliefs.

In the early 1990s, the government shifted its focus to social, economic and cultural restrictions aimed at blocking the development of Iran's Bahá'í community. Such measures included efforts to deprive Bahá'ís of their livelihood, to destroy their cultural heritage, and to prevent their young people from obtaining higher education.

Over the last several years, however, there has been a resurgence of more extreme forms of persecution directed at the 300,000-member Bahá'í community of Iran, that country's largest religious minority.

This upsurge has alarmed human rights monitors, who fear . . . that such attacks portend something far worse.

International experts on ethnic, racial or religious cleansing have identified a number of warning signs that often foreshadow widespread purges.

These include the "classification" of minority groups into categories of "us versus them," efforts to "dehumanize" them in the media and other venues, the organization of hate groups, and "preparation" for extermination. . . .

Ominously, a number of recent events in Iran fit into these categories.

Bahá'í International Community, "Executive Summary,"
The Bahá'í Question: Cultural Cleansing in Iran, *2008.*
www.news.bahai.org.

The Bahá'í faith was established in the mid-19th century by a Persian nobleman, Bahá'u'lláh, and expounds the spiritual unity of all mankind. The religion's five million members regard Bahá'ulláh as the latest in a line of prophets that includes Abraham, Moses, Buddha, Jesus and Mohammed.

Iran's Shiite religious establishment considers the religion a heretical offshoot of Islam.

Article 13 of the Iranian Constitution recognises only Jews, Christians and Zoroastrians as religious minorities in Iran, granting them representation in parliament and a degree of supervised and limited autonomy. Thus Bahá'ís have no legal rights and are not permitted to elect leaders of their community.

But despite this, said Ms. Ala'i, of the Bahá'í International Community, official discrimination has failed to "take root" among the public.

"People in Iran are more and more realising the injustices being done to their fellow citizens," she said, pointing to a recent public letter signed by 243 Iranians titled "We Are Ashamed," asking forgiveness "for the wrongs committed against the Bahá'í community of Iran".

And there are even signs the religious establishment is changing its outlook.

In May, Iranian Grand Ayatollah Hossein Ali Montazeri issued a fatwa [a legal pronouncement in Islam] stating that, "since [Bahá'ís] are the citizens of this country, they have the rights of a citizen and to live in this country".

"Furthermore, they must benefit from the Islamic compassion which is stressed in Qur'an and by the religious authorities."

India Struggles with Violence Caused by Forced Religious Conversions

Somini Sengupta

In the following viewpoint, Somini Sengupta reports on violence between Hindus and Christians in India. The violence began, according to Sengupta, when a popular Hindu preacher was killed, and his followers blamed Christians. Two groups, the Christian Panas and the Hindu Kandhas, have been at odds for years, with resentment for each other growing with the years, according to Sengupta. Hindu extremists have now begun forcing Christians to convert to Hinduism or face injury or death. Sengupta was the former New Delhi bureau chief for the New York Times, *where she is currently employed as a journalist.*

As you read, consider the following questions:

1. How many people were killed, houses burned, and churches destroyed in the violence described by Somini Sengupta in Orissa State, India?

2. How did men and women signal their embrace of Hinduism in their appearance?

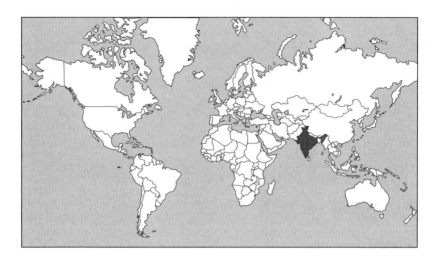

3. What happened to the Digal family after they told their story of forced conversion to a reporter, according to Sengupta?

The family of Solomon Digal was summoned by neighbors to what serves as a public square in front of the village tea shop.

They were ordered to get on their knees and bow before the portrait of a Hindu preacher. They were told to turn over their Bibles, hymnals and the two brightly colored calendar images of Christ that hung on their wall. Then, Digal, 45, a Christian since childhood, was forced to watch his Hindu neighbors set the items on fire.

"'Embrace Hinduism, and your house will not be demolished,'" Digal recalled being told on that Wednesday afternoon in September.

"'Otherwise, you will be killed, or you will be thrown out of the village.'"

Assault on the Freedom of Religion

India, the world's most populous democracy and officially a secular nation, is today haunted by a stark assault on one of its fundamental freedoms. Here in eastern Orissa State, riven by six weeks of religious clashes, Christian families like the Digals say they are being forced to abandon their faith in exchange for their safety.

The forced conversions come amid widening attacks on Christians here and in at least five other states across the country, as India prepares for national elections next spring.

> "In eastern Orissa State [India], riven by six weeks of religious clashes, Christian families . . . say they are being forced to abandon their faith for their safety."

The clash of faiths has brought panic and destruction throughout these once quiet hamlets fed by paddy fields and jackfruit trees. Here in Kandhamal, the district that has seen the greatest violence, more than 30 people have been killed, 3,000 homes burned and more than 130 churches destroyed, including the tin-roofed Baptist prayer hall where the Digals worshiped. Today it is a heap of rubble on an empty field, where cows blithely graze.

Across this ghastly terrain lie the singed remains of mud-and-thatch homes. Christian-owned businesses have been systematically attacked. Orange flags (orange is the sacred color of Hinduism) flutter triumphantly above the rooftops of houses and storefronts.

India is no stranger to religious violence between Christians, who make up about 2 percent of the population, and India's Hindu majority of 1.1 billion people. But this most recent spasm is the most intense in years.

It was set off, people here say, by the killing on Aug. 23 [2008] of a charismatic Hindu preacher known as Swami Laxmanananda Saraswati, who for 40 years had rallied the area's people to choose Hinduism over Christianity.

The police have blamed Maoist guerrillas for the swami's killing.

195

But Hindu radicals continue to hold Christians responsible.

In recent weeks, they have plastered these villages with gruesome posters of the swami's hacked corpse. "Who killed him?" the posters ask. "What is the solution?"

Tension Between the Panas and the Kandhas

Behind the clashes are long-simmering tensions between equally impoverished groups: the Panas and Kandhas. Both original inhabitants of the land, the two groups for ages worshiped the same gods.

Over the past several decades, the Panas for the most part became Christian, as Roman Catholic and Baptist missionaries arrived here more than 60 years ago, followed more recently by Pentecostals, who have proselytized more aggressively.

Meanwhile, the Kandhas, in part through the teachings of Laxmanananda, embraced Hinduism. The men tied the sacred Hindu white thread around their torsos; their wives daubed their foreheads with bright red vermilion. Temples sprouted.

Hate has been fed by economic tensions as well, as the government has categorized each tribe differently and given them different privileges.

"Hate has been fed by economic tensions as well, as the government has categorized each tribe [the Christian Panas and the Hindu Kandhas] differently and given them different privileges."

The Kandhas accused the Panas of cheating to obtain coveted quotas for government jobs. The Christian Panas, in turn, say their neighbors have become resentful as they have educated themselves and prospered.

Their grievances have erupted in sporadic clashes over the past 15 years, but they have exploded with a fury since the killing of Laxmanananda.

Two nights after his death, a Hindu mob in the village of Nuagaon dragged a Catholic priest and a nun from their residence, tore off much of their clothing and paraded them through the streets.

The nun told the police that she had been raped by four men, a charge the police say was borne out by a medical examination. Yet no one was arrested in the case until five weeks later, after a storm of media coverage. Today, five men are under arrest in connection with inciting the riots. The police say they are trying to find the nun and bring her back here to identify her attackers.

Given a chance to explain the recent violence, Subash Chauhan, the state's highest-ranking leader of Bajrang Dal, a Hindu radical group, described much of it as "a spontaneous reaction."

He said in an interview that the nun had not been raped but had had consensual sex.

On Sunday evening, as much of Kandhamal remained under curfew, Chauhan sat in the hall of a Hindu school in the state capital, Bhubaneshwar, beneath a huge portrait of the swami. A state police officer was assigned to protect him round the clock. He cupped a trilling BlackBerry in his hand.

"Hindu extremists have held ceremonies in the country's indigenous belt for the past several years designed to purge tribal communities of Christian influence."

Chauhan denied that his group was responsible for forced conversions and in turn accused Christian missionaries of luring villagers with incentives of schools and social services.

He was asked repeatedly whether Christians in Orissa should be left free to worship the god of their choice. "Why

---

The Cycle of Religious Violence in India

In the remote Indian state of Orissa your religion can cost you your life. Now a Christian mob has resorted to murder. Wielding knives and axes they have stabbed a Hindu man to death.

The killing followed a month-long campaign of murder, gang rape and arson by Hindu fanatics that drove Christians to take up arms to defend themselves, church officials in the area said yesterday. As many as 50,000 members of the minority Christian community have been forced into hiding in the jungle.

Rhys Blakely,
"India's Vengeful Christians Turn to Murder
as Hindus Step Up Their Killing Campaign,"
Times Online, September 27, 2008. www.timesonline.co.uk.

---

not?" he finally said, but he warned that it was unrealistic to expect the Kandhas to politely let their Pana enemies live among them as followers of Jesus.

"Who am I to give assurance?" he snapped. "Those who have exploited the Kandhas say they want to live together?"

Besides, he said, "they are Hindus by birth."

Forced Conversions

Hindu extremists have held ceremonies in the country's indigenous belt for the past several years designed to purge tribal communities of Christian influence.

It is impossible to know how many have been reconverted here, in the wake of the latest violence, though a three-day journey through the villages of Kandhamal turned up plenty of anecdotal evidence.

A few steps from where the nun had been raped in Nuagaon, five men, their heads freshly shorn, emerged from a soggy tent in a relief camp for Christians fleeing their homes.

The men had also been summoned to a village meeting in late August, where hundreds of their neighbors stood with machetes in hand and issued a firm order: Get your heads shaved and bow down before our gods, or leave this place.

Trembling with fear, Daud Nayak, 56, submitted to a shaving, a Hindu sign of sacrifice. He drank, as instructed, a tumbler of diluted cow dung, considered to be purifying.

In the eyes of his neighbors, he reckoned, he became a Hindu.

In his heart, he said, he could not bear it.

All five men said they fled the next day with their families. They refuse to return.

In another village, Birachakka, a man named Balkrishna Digal and his son, Saroj, said they had been summoned to a similar meeting and told by Hindu leaders who came from nearby villages that they, too, would have to convert. In their case, the ceremony was deferred because of rumors of Christian-Hindu clashes nearby.

For the time being, the family had placed an orange flag on their mud home. Their Hindu neighbors promised to protect them.

Here in Borepanga, the family of Solomon Digal was not so lucky.

Shortly after they recounted their Sept. 10 Hindu conversion story to a reporter in the dark of night, the Digals were again summoned by their neighbors. They were scolded and fined 501 rupees, or about $12, a pinching sum here.

The next morning, calmly clearing his cauliflower field, Lisura Paricha, one of the Hindu men who had summoned the Digals, confirmed that they had been penalized. Their crime, he said, was to talk to outsiders.

Religious Violence Still Plagues Northern Ireland

David McKittrick

In the following viewpoint, David McKittrick reports on the murder of two soldiers and a policeman in Northern Ireland in March 2009, using the event to reflect on Northern Ireland's troubled past. He argues that although the police force has been well integrated, sectarian violence between Protestants and Catholics continues. He also asserts that the society remains largely segregated in housing and education. He concludes that while it is likely that some sectarian violence will continue, many hope that it will not be reflective of the period between the 1960s and the 1990s. McKittrick is a journalist for the Independent.

As you read, consider the following questions:

1. When was the first sectarian riot in Belfast, according to David McKittrick?

2. What three men were pictured together walking down a flight of steps, illustrating a new policing era, according to McKittrick?

3. What percentage of children attend separate schools for Protestants and Catholics, according to McKittrick?

David McKittrick, "Northern Ireland: A Land Still Troubled by Its Past," *The Independent*, March 14, 2009. Copyright © 2009 Independent Newspapers (UK) Ltd. Reproduced by permission.

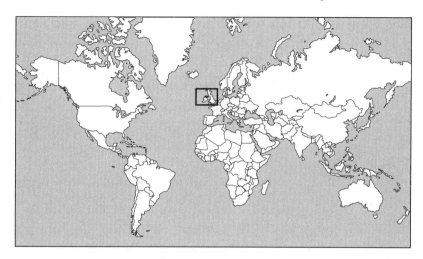

The scene at St. Therese's Catholic Church in Banbridge could have been an image from Northern Ireland 20 years ago. Silent crowds watching sombre lines of policemen marching behind the coffin of a fallen comrade. Grief-stricken members of the bereaved family comforting one another as the lone piper played a haunting lament.

But there was one big difference at the burial of PC Stephen Carroll yesterday. Two senior members of Sinn Féin were among the mourners, standing side-by-side with former loyalist paramilitaries. Behind the coffin walked the Commissioner of the Irish Garda alongside his counterpart from the Police Service of Northern Ireland (PSNI). All gestures unthinkable just a few years ago.

Thus the violent death and symbolic funeral of PC Carroll underlines the contradictions of the new "peace" in Northern Ireland—which has been both profound and patchy.

Another of these contradictions can be found in Belfast. There, in a tough loyalist ghetto in the north of the city, many parents have taken to sending their children to a religiously integrated school some distance away. They used to go to the nearby Protestant school, but instead the Protestant children are, for the first time, encountering Catholic kids and being educated with them. Yet this is not altogether a good news story.

> *"Although Northern Ireland has disappeared from the headlines in England because policemen and soldiers were not, until this week [March 2009], being killed, low-level violence has continued."*

The parents opting for integration are not motivated by a newfound instinct for religious harmony. Rather they are acting because they see their nearby school as being dominated by parents affiliated with another Protestant paramilitary group. Their children may benefit from the integration but not through any sense of reconciliation on the part of their parents.

Although Northern Ireland has disappeared from the headlines in England because policemen and soldiers were not, until this week, being killed, low-level violence has continued. A large proportion of the killings of the past decade resulted from savage feuding between loyalist groups like the Ulster Defence Association and the Ulster Volunteer Force.

Some widows do not wish to share a school with families whose members—they know or suspect—actually killed their husbands or partners. And so they self-segregate. In other districts, the children of UDA and UVF families do go to the same schools. But the mothers cluster in little factions at either end of the playground, glowering at each other.

On the republican side there has been less internecine violence but the rise of the Real IRA and Continuity IRA and the killings this last week prove that the threat remains. In 2007, dissident republicans shot and wounded one policeman and tried to blow up another in a car bomb. Last year they left a coffee jar bomb near a west Belfast police station (it failed to explode), rioted in Craigavon and shot dead another republican in an internal dispute. The famous statement of the Provisional IRA—"You need to get lucky every time, we only have to get lucky once"—still stands.

Thus the deaths this week raise the question of how peace is realistically to be defined. Because while the province has been improved immeasurably, the Troubles[1] still cast a long shadow. And history, ancient and modern, dictates that the peace will probably never be perfect.

A couple of centuries ago Belfast used to congratulate itself on being a reasonably peaceful little town, and on generally avoiding the sectarian disturbances which plagued Co Armagh. In fact Protestant citizens raised much of the money to pay for its first proper Catholic chapel: they even formed a guard of honour for the parish priest as he arrived to celebrate its first Mass. But things changed, partly because of those disturbances in Armagh. Protestant gangs there issued dire threats: "Now Teak this for Warnig, For if you Bee in this Contry Wednesday Night I will Blow your Soul to the Low hils of hell And Burn the House you are in."

"History, ancient and modern, dictates that the peace will probably never be perfect."

Seven thousand Catholics fled, many of them taking refuge in Belfast. This influx disturbed the religious balance there, and conflict ensued when the growing Catholic population brought competition for jobs and territory. The first sectarian riot came in 1813. The years that followed brought many clashes, often at the exact locations where rioting broke out during the most recent Troubles. Those sporadic riots went on, every few decades, right through the 20th century, though the recent Troubles were the worst and most sustained ever seen.

1. A period of ethnic and political violence in Northern Ireland, lasting from the 1960s until the Belfast Agreement of 1998.

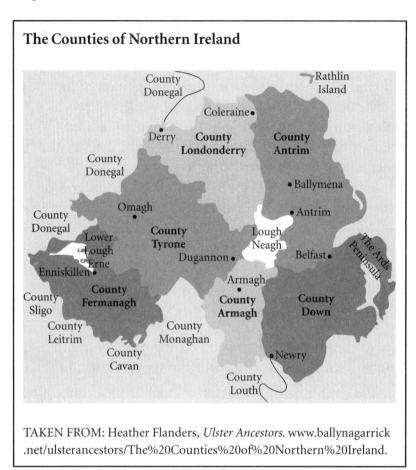

The Counties of Northern Ireland

TAKEN FROM: Heather Flanders, *Ulster Ancestors*. www.ballynagarrick
.net/ulsterancestors/The%20Counties%20of%20Northern%20Ireland.

The Troubles erupted in the late 1960s when Catholics took to the streets campaigning for improved civil rights. The reaction of the police was a highly divisive element. The Royal Ulster Constabulary was internationally condemned for over-reaction as its members wielded batons against peaceful marchers.

The memory of the decades of killings that ensued makes one wince, and huge problems persist. But 40 years on Northern Ireland can—miraculously—be described as a fair society. The old system of Protestant domination has gone.

Most of the initial civil rights demands have been dealt with to general satisfaction and are long gone from the political agenda. Effective laws mean that employers who discriminate are hit where it hurts most, in the pocket. The old bastions of Protestant employment no longer pose a problem—some, such as the famous shipyards, because there are hardly any jobs there any more.

Others, like the once unbalanced civil service, now have an equitable workforce. Professor Bob Osborne, of the University of Ulster, summed it up: "In many areas Catholics have caught up with or surpassed Protestants, and there is no longer consistent Catholic relative disadvantage to the same degree as in the 1970s and 1980s. It is unusual to find such a rate of social change within a generation—it is quite dramatic."

Protestant politicians such as the First Minister Peter Robinson are served by staff of both religions. And of course Martin McGuinness of Sinn Féin is the number two man in government. During the past week things held together because the police service is no longer viewed as a Protestant preserve. Both sides can identify with it, which is why Mr. McGuinness branded as "traitors" those who killed one of its members.

The PSNI has replaced the RUC, and policing has been given the most radical overhaul. The old system of segregation, where one community effectively policed the other, has ended. The PSNI now has many more Catholics in the ranks but more importantly it has been festooned with so many oversight bodies that it is described as possibly the world's most scrutinised police service.

"There is still a level of violence which is non-terrorist but sectarian."

Sometimes all this supervision is criticised as excessive, yet the value of the insistence on accountability was this week seen in a single image which will be remembered in Belfast as symbolising a huge turning point. This was when the PSNI's Chief Constable Sir Hugh Orde was pictured walking down a flight of steps, flanked by Mr. Robinson and Mr. McGuinness. Nothing could have better illustrated the emergence of a new policing era with a service acceptable to almost everyone. A sense of common purpose emerged.

Reforms in policing have been tried many times before in the history of the north of Ireland, yet this is the first time they have actually worked to produce a system which commands support across the board. As this week showed, policing is no longer a source of contention but commands cross-community support. It used to be said of Northern Ireland that the centre cannot hold: this time it has.

But although one part of the age-old patterns has been transformed from a negative into a positive, many unfortunate features remain. There is still a level of violence which is non-terrorist but sectarian. In many places outside Belfast, people refer to "the Catholic end of the town", talk about "the other side", and inquire about religion by asking, "What foot does he kick with?" (Protestants are said to kick with the right, Catholics with the left.) Many people claim they can identify one of "the other sort" simply by looking at them.

Much of this can be relatively harmless but in some places it can be deeply unsettling and on occasion it can be lethal. The predominantly Protestant town of Ballymena in Co Antrim, for instance, has long had a reputation for sectarianism.

It has its attractions: outsiders flock there for the shopping and its old-fashioned little streets. Yet its recent history makes the point that in Northern Ireland peace is a relative concept. In this town of less than 30,000 people, police in one recent 12-month period recorded 133 sectarian incidents. For some of Ballymena's youth, skirmishes with "the other sort" are part of their lives.

Sometimes they can lose those lives. Three years ago, Michael McIlveen, a 15-year-old Catholic, was cornered in an alley by Protestant youths who battered him to death. A few weeks ago three young men, who had been teenagers at the time, were convicted of murder.

That incident took place in the post-Troubles era, yet it and many others make the unpalatable point that Northern Ireland has rarely been fully at peace. A glance at newspaper archives for supposedly quiet times reveals a picture of an intrinsically restless society. Many now hazily remember the pre-Troubles early 1960s as something of a golden age of peace and potential progress but in fact there were dozens of cases of riots, arson and street clashes.

An ice cream van at a Protestant rally was surrounded and attacked when a rumour spread that the driver was Catholic. A Unionist MP who made a speech advocating toleration was dragged from his platform and battered unconscious.

A Catholic woman, now in her 70s, recalled how, as a teenager in a small and predominantly Protestant Co Armagh town, she was asked by a local Protestant doctor why she did not play table tennis with young Protestants in the local Orange hall. When she said she did not believe she would be welcome he persuaded her to go along, saying: "Nonsense, you're being silly." She recounted: "I had a great evening but the next day the doctor came to me, all embarrassed, and said: 'I'm really sorry about this, but they've asked me to tell you not to come back.' He was shocked and embarrassed. I never forgot that."

The two communities worship apart and are generally schooled apart. An integrated education movement has been struggling gamely on for decades, but more than 90 percent of children still attend separate schools. The universities look completely integrated but actually are affected by a degree of self-segregation. A senior academic who came in from abroad was dismayed to discover that Protestant students tended to congregate in one canteen, Catholics in another.

It is too early to say whether the peace process will counteract the tendency for many Protestant teenagers to go to universities in England and Scotland, and to find jobs there instead of returning home. The pattern has become so ingrained that it has generated its own jocular acronym, Nipples, standing for Northern Ireland Protestant Professionals Living in England and Scotland.

Yet as the revelries on the streets of the university area show, many of Belfast's students have the traditional undergraduate interest in sex, drink and rock 'n' roll. While this has led to quite a few mixed marriages, these are almost always conducted in conditions of secrecy due to social and indeed security difficulties. Since working-class housing is almost entirely segregated, the question of finding somewhere safe to live is a highly delicate one.

The same secrecy was recently outlined privately by a Catholic priest whose parish includes a large, entirely Protestant estate: at least everyone, including the priest, thought it was entirely Protestant. It was only when a parishioner died that he discovered some Catholics lived there. They were so cautious and discreet that, instead of going to Mass locally, they travel weekly to another church miles away to keep their religion unknown.

Since the killing rate has fallen there has been a huge sense of security easing: many have gone to places they have never gone to before. But no peacelines have come down and efforts to integrate housing are tentative. This is not an ideal way to live, yet life has been so much better than in the years of violence that most relished the improvement and in many ways settled for it.

This week, with the deaths of two soldiers and a policeman everyone re-checked their level of security. Police officers in particular are locking up their homes, checking their cars and reverting to the old ways of varying their routines.

Some people have stopped taking short-cuts through dubious areas. Some will opt to stay home rather than go out this weekend; those who do venture out will think carefully about which pubs they should go to.

No one knows if the republican dissidents who carried out the killings will strike again; no one knows whether loyalist extremists will exact revenge. But the new element in this, the latest of so many security crises, was that the body politic has so far proved cohesive, determined and united in asserting that the police are now everyone's police.

Mr. Robinson and Mr. McGuinness have gone for St Patrick's Day to the States, where they will meet Barack Obama and, standing side by side with him, produce another symbolic image of the new unity of old opponents.

"History and geography dictate that Northern Ireland is never going to be a tranquil, placid place. There is still much division around, but it coexists with hope and a determination not to return to the bad old days."

Back home, it is evident that the society they represent remains physically divided, containing as it does two separate communities. Yet historic breakthroughs have been made. The police service has been successfully integrated into all of society, as it has never been over the centuries.

And politicians have achieved a striking measure of top-down integration: Mr. Robinson and Mr. McGuinness are both figures from the bad old days, but these one-time warriors have now turned into heroes of the peace process. The hope is that the model of cooperation they have established will gradually trickle down into the divided society, for in political terms they have displayed a degree of political integration most had never thought possible.

History and geography dictate that Northern Ireland is never going to be a tranquil, placid place. There is still much division around, but it coexists with hope and a determination not to return to the bad old days.

The prospects were once summed up in advice by the former US senator George Mitchell: "This has been centuries in the making; it will be years in the changing."

World Religious Leaders Work for Peace in South Asia

World Council of Churches, Christian Conference of Asia, and South Asian Councils of Churches

The following viewpoint is a statement issued by the World Council of Churches (WCC), Christian Conference of Asia (CCA), and South Asian Councils of Churches (SACC) regarding peace, security and development in South Asia. The group argues that South Asia is becoming increasingly unstable due to religious and ethnic extremism, and the intervention of major world powers in the region. The group urges churches throughout the world, and particularly in South Asia, to work together to build peace and end violence. The WCC, CCA, and SACC are ecumenical Christian fellowship bodies composed of churches worldwide. Founded in 1948, the World Council of Churches is now a fellowship of more than 340 Christian churches confessing together "the Lord Jesus Christ according to the scriptures" and seeking "to fulfill together their common calling to the glory of the one God, Father, Son and Holy Spirit". Tracing its origins to international movements dedicated to world mission and evangelism, life and work, faith and order, Christian education and church unity, the World Council is made up primarily of Protes-

World Council of Churches, Christian Conference of Asia, and South Asian Councils of Churches, "Statement of the International Consultation on Peace, Security and Development in South Asia," The World Council of Churches, April 2, 2009. Copyright © World Council of Churches. Reproduced by permission.

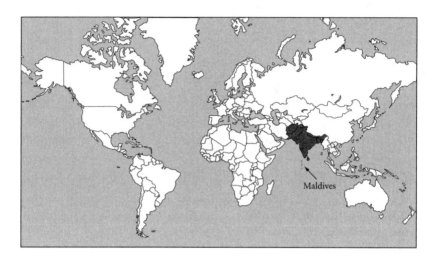

tant and Orthodox churches. The Roman Catholic Church is not a member church but participates with the World Council of Churches and its member communions in a variety of activities and dialogues.

As you read, consider the following questions:

1. How many foreign forces are in Afghanistan and what has their presence created, according to the viewpoint?
2. Which five nations does the viewpoint name as having undergone democratic electoral processes?
3. Where and when did WCC, CCA, and SACC hold their international consultation on Peace, Security and Development in South Asia?

South Asia continues to be one of the most volatile regions of the world. The negative effects of ongoing ethnic conflicts, civil wars, ethnic cleansing, communal and political violence, terrorism, counterterrorism, religious extremism, militarization, gross and systematic violation of human rights, unresolved inter-state and intra-state conflicts, and subversive economic interests, etc., are visible today more than ever before in the region. South Asia has become a hotbed of the war on terror and a victim of the strategic interests of major power blocs keeping the region in constant turmoil and uncertainty. The nature of its volatility and that of the conflicts has been redefined by the U.S.-led war on terror, wherein the rulers of the region have joined together as partners. This has wider repercussions in the region as resentments against foreign forces in the region are growing among various sectors in society, especially as they feel that peace and security in South Asia are today defined in terms of American strategic interests and objectives. Home to one fifth of the world's population, this region is accountable for fifty percent of the world's illiterate and forty percent of the world's poor. This poverty stricken region faces the worst hit of innumerable adversities in terms of securing peace, security and development. The extent of human deprivation in the region contrasts with the large armies, modern weapons and increasing defense budgets, arms race, and nuclear power struggle, which keep the region seething with growing unrest. The criminalisation of politics and corruption undermine the democratic principles of the electoral system.

Violence Throughout the Region

While the 25-year-old ethnic conflict and civil war in Sri Lanka reaches its climax, the country faces a continuously worsening humanitarian crisis exceeding all imaginable proportions. Tens of thousands of civilians are trapped by the war in the northern war zone. According to the UN [Office of the] High Commissioner for Human Rights, around 180,000 people are trapped in the war zone amidst shelling and crossfire, lacking basic amenities such as food, medicine, shelter, sanitation, etc. There are disturbing reports of the conditions inside the camps in which those who have come out of the war zone are confined. At the same time, the country faces the emergence of religious intolerance and extremism.

Although the International Security Assistance Force (ISAF) is engaged in counterterrorism in Afghanistan, the overwhelming presence and reliance on 52,000-strong foreign forces in Afghanistan has created more animosity among the local people as well as in neighbouring Pakistan. This situation creates an atmosphere ripe for extremist groups to exploit the religious sentiments of ordinary people and involve them in committing more violence. Today, Afghanistan is plagued by a new insurgency, and a deep humanitarian crisis prevails in the country. This warrants a situation where we must step forward with assistance to strengthen areas of governance, rule of law, democratic institutions and reconstruction of the country. Pakistan is buffeted by numerous and serious crises and is still in the grip of political crisis, growing religious fundamentalism, and terrorism. The continuous terrorist attacks, clashes between security forces and militants, military operations, political violence, inter-tribe sectarian clashes and border clashes are the biggest threat to the state and citizens of Pakistan. India, the largest democracy in the world, faces serious threats to its peace, security and development. Religious intolerance and the politicisation of religion, the persecution of minorities, and [the] criminalisation of politics have become increasing trends in India today. India's long cherished religious tolerance and secular values have been threatened by religious fundamentalists. The constitutional rights to profess and propagate their faith granted to all citizens are threatened. The attacks on Christians in Kandhamal, Orissa, and Karnataka, and sporadic violence against religious minorities in other parts of India are causes of serious concern as the incidents build walls of separation and hatred between communities and people. The democratic transition in Bangladesh in the recent election gave much hope to the people of Bangladesh. However, the emerging trend of religious extremism and fundamentalism and also the recent trend of dissatisfaction among the military forces are serious concerns, as they could derail the democratic governance in the country.

"India's long cherished religious tolerance and secular values have been threatened by religious fundamentalists."

Hope in Turbulent Times

While these problems menace peace, security and development in the region in various ways, there are certain silver linings which provide hope amidst these turbulent times in the history of the South Asian countries. All South Asian countries have undergone democratic transitions and electoral processes in recent times. Countries such as Bhutan, Nepal, the Maldives, Bangladesh, and Pakistan have undergone democratic electoral processes. Following 100 years of rule by absolute monarchy, the Himalayan kingdom of Bhutan shifted to democracy. After having experienced deadly armed conflicts for a decade, Nepal ended its centuries-old monarchy and has undergone a series of transformations which are shaping it as a federal democratic republic. In the midst of increasing violence and the military's highhandedness in Pakistan, the world has witnessed the victory of the people's power in the fight against authoritarianism, and the struggle of civil society mobilisation for the restoration of an independent judiciary. The Maldives has ended its one man dictatorship and the first democratic government in three decades was established in a multi-party election recently. After several years of political turmoil and two years of a military-supported caretaker administration, the outcome of the election process in the country has further re-enforced the hope of political order returning to Bangladesh.

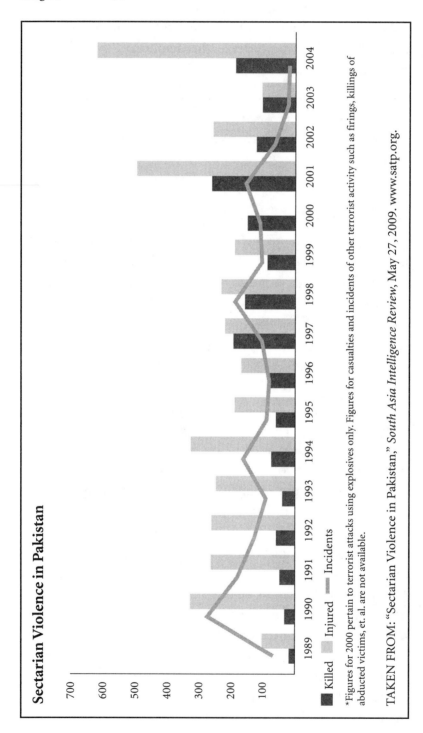

Sectarian Violence in Pakistan

■ Killed ▨ Injured ━ Incidents

*Figures for 2000 pertain to terrorist attacks using explosives only. Figures for casualties and incidents of other terrorist activity such as firings, killings of abducted victims, et. al. are not available.

TAKEN FROM: "Sectarian Violence in Pakistan," *South Asia Intelligence Review,* May 27, 2009. www.satp.org.

Church Organizations Take Action

Concerned by the alarming situation affecting the South Asian countries and its manifold impacts on nurturing peace, security and development, and despite initiatives from different quarters of society and different national, diplomatic and ecumenical interventions, the World Council of Churches (WCC), the Christian Conference of Asia (CCA), and the South Asian Councils of Churches (SACC) organised an International Consultation on Peace, Security and Development in South Asia, which was held at Whitefield, Bangalore from 30 March to 2 April 2009.

The Consultation was aimed at exploring: possibilities of hope amidst desperation; assuring solidarity and support to the suffering people of South Asia; accompanying the churches in the region in their mission and prophetic witness to uphold the values of peace with justice; and assisting them in exploring interventions that could bring peace, reconciliation, security and development to this volatile region.

South Asian church and ecumenical leaders, together with representatives from churches from the WCC and CCA constituencies in different Asian countries and ecumenical development and relief/humanitarian aid agencies from Europe and North America, attended the consultation and agreed that the grave humanitarian crisis—threat to peace and security in South Asia—are a challenge not only to the churches, but also to the conscience of the international community. Having listened to and realised the seriousness of the situation in various South Asian countries, the WCC-CCA-SACC Consultation:

- *Condemns* all forms of terrorism both by state and non-state actors in the South Asia region;

- *Calls* upon all parties concerned to eschew violence and invest in negotiated settlements of all issues which will ensure peace, security and development in the region;

- *Expresses* concern over the emerging religious extremism and fundamentalism in all South Asian countries;

- *Expresses* deep concern over the continuously worsening humanitarian crisis in the northern parts of Sri Lanka;

- *Appeals* to the Sri Lankan government and the LTTE [the Liberation Tigers of Tamil Eelam, a separatist organization] to immediately stop the ongoing military operations to ensure safe passage arranged by credible and neutral agencies for those who are trapped in the war zone;

- *Urges* the LTTE to facilitate safe conduct for the people who want to leave such areas and refrain from any form of forced conscription, of both children and others;

- *Appeals* to the Sri Lankan government to allow international and national agencies to address and assist the persons in camps and in the conflict areas;

- *Urges* the Sri Lankan government to take initiatives conducive to undertaking talks with all concerned and also to present an outline of a political formula with a view to finding a lasting solution to the issues behind the conflict;

- *Assures* the churches in Sri Lanka of the support of the churches around the world, represented by the WCC, the CCA and the SACC, as they are engaged in responding to the urgent humanitarian needs and also in working with others in seeking practical ways of resolving the conflict;

- *Congratulates* the people of Nepal for achieving peace and democracy through a long and united struggle and urges all political actors in Nepal to make every effort to complete the historical task of drafting the new constitution of the federal democratic republic of Nepal within the stipulated time frame;

- *Welcomes* the democratic transformation in Bhutan and the constitutional guarantees for religious freedom in the country;

- *Calls* for the withdrawal of U.S.-led international combat troops from Afghanistan and appeals to the international community to ensure that the resultant power vacuum may be filled by a UN-sponsored peacekeeping force with Asian forces as major players, which will help the country's transition towards stability;

- *Urges* the Churches and national ecumenical councils in the region, together with the WCC, CCA and SACC to undertake measures that will capacitate in mitigating the suffering of the civilians who are facing threats to their life, property and resources, to equip their constituents in skills of conflict transformation, while at the same time lobbying with their respective governments to work towards the restoration of peace in all South Asian countries and in the region.

"The [World Council of Churches-Christian Conference of Asia-South Asian Councils of Churches] Consultation . . . expresses concern over the emerging religious extremism and fundamentalism in all South Asian Countries."

Within the context of this turbulent period in the history of South Asia, when situations of war and conflict, killings and the massacre of innocent civilians are pervasive in people's daily lives in South Asia, the ecumenical movement and churches are challenged to be instruments of God's peace and reconciliation. They are called to revisit their witness and mission to strengthen a sense of belonging in God's reconciling world. The people of God in South Asia, together with their accompaniers from around the globe, are encouraged to work towards peace, security and reconciliation which will ultimately ensure the fullness of life for all.

Periodical Bibliography

The following articles have been selected to supplement the diverse views presented in this chapter.

Barbara Amiel   "School Heads Are 'Enablers' of Anti-Semitism," *Maclean's*, vol. 122, no. 16, May 4, 2009.

Economist   "The Muslims and Christians of Jos, Nigeria," December 6, 2008.

Paul Freston and Virginia Garrard-Burnett   "Christianity and Conflict in Latin America," National Defense University and Pew Forum Symposium, April 6, 2006. www.pewforum.org.

Ahmad Fauzi Abdul Hamid   "Islam and Violence in Malaysia," S. Rajaratnam School of International Studies Working Paper, March 2007. www.isn.ethz.ch.

Yong Huey Jiun   "Harness Religions to Promote Justice, Peace," *Straits Times*, July 19, 2008.

Rien Kuntari   "Cartoon of Prophet Debate in the Internet Age: Indonesia Case," The Oxford Center for Religion and Public Life, 2008.

Jonathan Manthorpe   "Previous Attacks Aimed to Stir Up Muslim-Hindu Violence," *Vancouver Sun*, November 26, 2008.

Ola Mohamed   "Religion and Violence," *Faith Divide—On Faith at The Washington Post*, April 15, 2009. http://newsweek.washingtonpost.com.

Arvind Narrain and Clifton D'Rozario   "The Bogey of Forced Conversions," *Hindu*, October 26, 2008. www.hinduonnet.com.

Adianto P. Simamora   "Religious Violence Getting Worse in Indonesia," *Jakarta Post*, January 14, 2009. www.asianewsnet.net.

For Further Discussion

Chapter 1

1. According to the viewpoints in this chapter, what world religions are experiencing growth? What religions are in decline? Compare and contrast the characteristics of the growing religions with those that are in decline. Why do you think the memberships are changing?

2. Several of the authors of the viewpoints in this chapter are concerned with increasing understanding among peoples of different religions. What do you think are the most important actions people of goodwill can take to ensure harmony among differing religious groups? Use examples from the viewpoints to support your answer.

Chapter 2

1. Science and religion have different ways of explaining the world and use different sources of knowledge, according to the writers of this chapter. Why has the conflict between science and religion escalated in recent years? Do you think there is a place for both science and religion? If so, why? If not, why not?

2. Summarize the basic difference between the beliefs of evolutionists and creationists, according to the writers in this chapter. Who makes the more convincing case? Do you think that creationism ought to be taught in schools alongside evolution? Why or why not?

Chapter 3

1. According to the authors of this chapter, the freedom of speech and the freedom of religion are fundamental rights in many countries of the world. In what ways do these

two rights sometimes come into conflict? Do you think one should take precedence over the other, and if so, why?

2. Should governments protect members of religious groups from defamation even if it means curtailing freedom of speech for other citizens? What examples of this do you see in the viewpoints in this chapter?

Chapter 4

1. The Dalai Lama and the Chinese government offer very different explanations about violence in Tibet. Which viewpoint do you find more reasonable and why?

2. The writers in this chapter explore many different facets of religious violence. Why do you think religion has been the cause of so much violence in history? What can, or should, be done to curb religious violence?

Organizations to Contact

The editors have compiled the following list of organizations concerned with the issues debated in this book. The descriptions are derived from materials provided by the organizations. All have publications or information available for interested readers. The list was compiled on the date of publication of the present volume; the information provided here may change. Be aware that many organizations take several weeks or longer to respond to inquiries, so allow as much time as possible.

Christian Solidarity Worldwide (CSW)
PO Box 99, New Malden, Surrey
 KT3 3YF
 United Kingdom
+44(0)-8454565464 • fax: +44(0)-2089428802
Web site: www.csw.org.uk

Christian Solidarity Worldwide (CSW) is a human rights advocacy organization working on behalf of Christians worldwide who are persecuted for their beliefs. The organization's Web site includes press releases, news articles, and special publications such as *No Place to Call Home*, a report that studies what happens to Muslims who choose to leave their faith. Other publications include *Aftermath of Anti-Christian Violence in Orissa State, India*; *Peru: Fact Finding and Advocacy Visit Report*; and *Nepal—Toward Peace, Democracy and Religious Freedom*.

Hartford Institute for Religion Research
Hartford Seminary, Hartford, CT   06105-2260
(860) 509-9543 • fax: (860) 509-9551
e-mail: hirr@hartsem.edu
Web site: www.hartfordinstitute.org

The Hartford Institute for Religion Research is an educational and research organization that focuses on issues of practical theology, denominations, and the sociology of religion. The group maintains an active Web site that includes book excerpts, religion data, bibliographies, and current articles. Sample publications on its Web site include the 2009 *Not Who You Think They Are: A Profile of People Who Attend America's Megachurches* and a fact sheet, "Quick Information About U.S. Religious Life."

Human Rights Without Frontiers International (HRWF)
Avenue Winston Churchill 11/331180, Brussels
  Belgium
+32-234556145
e-mail: international.secretariat.brussels@hrwf.net
Web site: www.hrwf.net

Human Rights Without Frontiers International (HRWF) is a nongovernmental organization with offices worldwide. According to its Web site, the focus of the HRWF's activities is "monitoring, research, and analysis on the field of human rights as well as the promotion of democracy." The organization also focuses on freedom of religion and belief. HRWF includes publications such as *Profiles of Religious, Spiritual, and Philosophical Entities*, which describes the various religious organizations around the world including Christian Science, Moon, and Hare Krishna, and a news archive on its Web site.

The Office of His Holiness the 14th Dalai Lama
Thekchen Choeling, HP, Dharamsala
  176219
  India
91-1892221343 • fax: 91-1892221879
e-mail: ohhdl@dalailama.com
Web site: www.dalailama.com

The Office of His Holiness the 14th Dalai Lama is the personal office of the Tibetan religious and political leader, His Holiness the Dalai Lama. The organization provides secretarial assistance to the Dalai Lama, organizes his schedule, handles all diplomatic correspondence, and acts as liaison between the Dalai Lama and the officials of the Tibetan Government-in-

Exile. The office's Web site includes information regarding Tibetan Buddhism and a biography of the Dalai Lama, along with his teachings, messages, and speeches. It also includes photographs, Web casts, and the latest news concerning the Dalai Lama, Buddhism, and the Tibetan Government-in-Exile.

The Office of International Religious Freedom

U.S. Department of State, Washington, DC   20520
(220) 647-4000
Web site: www.state.gov/g/drl/irf

The Office of International Religious Freedom has the mission of promoting religious freedom as a core objective of U.S. foreign policy. The office publishes *The Annual Report on International Religious Freedom*, a book that is available online through the Web site. The Web site also includes archives of international religious freedom testimony before U.S. Congress, videos of key speeches by the secretary of state, and articles.

Ontario Consultants on Religious Tolerance (OCRT)

PO Box 27026, Kingston, Ontario
  K7M 8W5
  Canada
fax: (613) 547-9015
Web site: www.religioustolerance.org

The goal of the Ontario Consultants on Religious Tolerance is to provide a clear and unbiased description of worldwide religions, beliefs, and practices. Its Web site includes mainstream and little-known religions and has over 4,800 essays on controversial subjects such as abortion, homosexuality, and same-sex marriage.

Organisation of the Islamic Conference

PO Box 178, Jeddah   21411
  Kingdom of Saudi Arabia
+966-26900001 • fax: +966-22751953
Web site: www.oic-oci.org

According to the Organisation of the Islamic Conference's Web site, it is the second largest intergovernmental organization after the United Nations. Its mission is to be the collective voice of Muslims throughout the world. The group also monitors Islamophobia (prejudice or discrimination against Islam or Muslims) around the world. The organization provides publications, news articles, and a comprehensive media library on its Web site. Sample publications include *2008 Hate Crime Survey: Violence Against Muslims* and *Combating Intolerance and Discrimination Against Muslims.*

Pew Forum on Religion & Public Life

1615 L Street NW, Suite 700, Washington, DC 20036-5610
(202) 419-4550 • fax: (202) 419-4559
Web site: http://pewforum.org

According to its Web site, the Pew Forum on Religion & Public Life "seeks to promote a deeper understanding of issues at the intersection of religion and public affairs." The forum acts as a clearinghouse of information and a research center. Its Web site offers surveys, legal backgrounders, articles, transcripts, and debates on controversial issues.

Tzu Chi Foundation

U.S.A. National Headquarters, San Dimas, CA 91773-3728
(909) 447-7799 • fax: (909) 447-7948
e-mail: info@us.tzuchi.org
Web site: www.us.tzuchi.org

The Tzu Chi Foundation is a nonprofit, volunteer-based, service organization for Buddhists. Representatives of the foundation offer humanitarian aid to people all over the world who are beset with problems such as poverty and national disasters. In addition to explanations about Buddhism and Tzu Chi, its Web site also offers publications such as the *Tzu Chi USA Journal* and *The World of Tzu Chi*; daily speeches from the founder, Dharma Master Cheng Yen; photographs of Tzu Chi work; and news reports.

World Council of Churches (WCC)

150 route de Ferney, Geneva 2   1211
   Switzerland
+41-227916111 • fax: +41-227910361
Web site: www.oikoumene.org

The World Council of Churches (WCC) is a large international organization of over three hundred Christian churches and denominations, representing more than 560 million Christians worldwide. The WCC describes itself as inclusive and ecumenical, meaning that it welcomes people from diverse Christian backgrounds. The group publishes articles and books, available through its Web site. Its Web site also includes news briefs on current situations affecting Christians around the world.

Bibliography of Books

Jason C. Bivins	*Religion of Fear: The Politics of Horror in Conservative Evangelicalism.* New York: Oxford University Press, 2008.
Adam Yuet Chau	*Miraculous Response: Doing Popular Religion in Contemporary China.* Stanford, CA: Stanford University Press, 2006.
Peter Clarke	*New Religions in Global Perspective: Religious Change in the Modern World.* New York: Routledge, 2006.
Juan Ricardo Cole	*Engaging the Muslim World.* New York: Palgrave Macmillan, 2009.
Thomas Crean	*God Is No Delusion: A Refutation of Richard Dawkins.* Ft. Collins, CO: Ignatius Press, 2007.
Noel Davies and Martin Conway	*World Christianity in the Twentieth Century: A Reader.* London: SCM Press, 2008.
Richard Dawkins	*The God Delusion.* New York: Houghton Mifflin, 2006.
Ilia Delio	*Christ in Evolution.* Maryknoll, NY: Orbis Books, 2008.
E.J. Dionne	*Souled Out: Reclaiming Faith and Politics After the Religious Right.* Princeton, NJ: Princeton University Press, 2008.

Thomas Dixon · *Science and Religion: A Very Short Introduction.* New York: Oxford University Press, 2008.

Steve Fuller · *Dissent over Descent: Intelligent Design's Challenge to Darwinism.* Thriplow, Cambridge: Icon, 2008.

H. Wayne House · *Intelligent Design 101: Leading Experts Explain the Key Issues.* Grand Rapids, MI: Kregel Publications, 2008.

Pico Iyer · *The Open Road: The Global Journey of the Fourteenth Dalai Lama.* New York: Alfred A. Knopf, 2008.

Susan Jacoby · *The Age of American Unreason.* New York: Pantheon Books, 2008.

Brendan January · *The Iranian Revolution.* Minneapolis, MN: Twenty-First Century Books, 2008.

Blaine Kaltman · *Under the Heel of the Dragon: Islam, Racism, Crime and the Uighur in China.* Athens, OH: Ohio University Press, August 28, 2007.

Stuart A. Kauffman · *Reinventing the Sacred: A New View of Science, Reason, and Religion.* New York: Basic Books, 2008.

Timothy J. Keller · *The Reason for God: Belief in an Age of Skepticism.* New York: Dutton, 2008.

Bernard Lewis · *Islam: The Religion and the People.* Indianapolis, IN: Wharton Press, 2009.

Brenda J. Lutz and James M. Lutz	*Global Terrorism.* Los Angeles: SAGE Publications, 2008.
Kenneth R. Miller	*Only a Theory: Evolution and the Battle for America's Soul.* New York: Viking Penguin, 2008.
Jacob Neusner	*World Religions in America: An Introduction.* Louisville, KY: Westminster John Knox Press, 2009.
Andrew Newberg	*How God Changes Your Brain: Breakthrough Findings from a Leading Neuroscientist.* New York: Ballantine Books, 2009.
Martha Craven Nussbaum	*Liberty of Conscience: In Defense of American's Tradition of Religious Equality.* New York: Basic Books, 2008.
Dean L. Overman	*A Case for the Existence of God.* Lanham, MD: Rowman & Littlefield, 2009.
John Powers	*A Concise Introduction to Tibetan Buddhism.* Ithaca, NY: Snow Lion Publications, 2008.
Arvind Sharma	*The World's Religions After September 11.* Westport, CT: Praeger, 2009.
Russell Shorto	*Descartes' Bones: A Skeletal History of the Conflict Between Faith and Reason.* New York: Doubleday, 2008.

Rodney Stark	*What Americans Really Believe: New Findings from the Baylor Surveys of Religion*. Waco, TX: Baylor University Press, 2008.
Sharon R. Steadman	*The Archaeology of Religion: Cultures and Their Beliefs in Worldwide Context*. Walnut Creek, CA: Left Coast Press, 2009.
Victoria Kennick Urubshurow	*Introducing World Religions*. New York: Routledge, 2008.
David J. Wolpe	*Why Faith Matters*. New York: HarperOne, 2008.
Phil Zuckerman	*Society Without God: What the Least Religious Nations Can Tell Us About Contentment*. New York: New York University Press, 2008.

Index

I